House Beautiful

Your Dream Home

House Beautiful

Your Dream Home

LISA S. SIGLAG

Hearst Books

A Division of Sterling Publishing Co., Inc.
New York

Library of Congress Cataloging-in-Publication Data avaliable

10 9 8 7 6 5 4 3 2 1

Designed by Patricia Fabricant

Published by Hearst Books
A Division of Sterling Publishing Co., Inc.
387 Park Avenue South, New York, NY 10016

House Beautiful and Hearst Books are trademarks of Hearst Communications, Inc.

www.housebeautiful.com

For information about custom editions, special sales, premium and corporate purchases, please contact Sterling Special Sales Department at 800-805-5489 or specialsales@sterlingpub.com.

Distributed in Canada by Sterling Publishing
C/o Canadian Manda Group, 165 Dufferin Street
Toronto, Ontario, Canada M6K 3H6

Distributed in Australia by Capricorn Link (Australia) Pty. Ltd.
P.O. Box 704, Windsor, NSW 2756 Australia

Manufactured in China

Sterling ISBN 13: 978-1-58816-470-4
          ISBN 10: 1-58816-470-5

PAGE 1: Selecting only a few pieces of furniture affords a very streamlined look. Textures in the oversized seats and finely woven carpet offer visual interest and warm up the living room.

PAGE 2: Flooring should be as durable as it is beautiful. Here, a limestone floor adds cool elegance to this spacious contemporary living room. Be sure to consider cleaning and care when you're researching flooring options.

Contents

CHAPTER ONE

Before You Begin

The owners of this residence worked closely with their architect to design a vacation home rooted in the New England vernacular. Wide doorways allow a continuous flow of space throughout the house. Here, a salvaged wood lintel holds court above two cypress doors.

Hiring a Team of Professionals

Welcome to the world of home design, where even details have details. For a project to be a success, be it building an 8,000-square-foot home or adding a powder room, it's crucial to assemble a team of professionals who will offer support and guidance. This group of experts will give shape and form to your new home. You'll need to have confidence in each individual you hire, admire his work, and feel comfortable discussing budgets and timelines.

The best way to find an expert is through friends and family. Ask around for names of contractors, architects, and designers. You can also check a variety of organizations to find a pro. Below and on the pages that follow, you'll find an explanation of what each type of expert does, how each charges, and specific design organizations that provide information on locating a specialist.

LEFT: Set on Martha's Vineyard, the summerhouse is new construction, but you can barely tell. The builder designed it to appear as though it had been there since the 1920s.

OPPOSITE: Inside this shingle-style house, spaces flow into one another. Large, unadorned windows let in natural light from all sides, giving the house an open and airy feeling.

- ARCHITECT: Architects work with the entire scope of the project, from designing a space to ensuring that it is structurally sound to specifying materials and products. Architects are also knowledgeable about building codes and zoning laws. Generally, your architect will work with you to plan the new space, submitting several sets of drawings for your approval, concluding with a final set of construction plans that give the contractor detailed specifications, from room dimensions to product placement.

You can also ask your architect to oversee construction, for a fee, but more often the architect's job will end with approval of final plans, though he or she may help you find and hire a contractor. Architects' fees can vary

BEFORE YOU BEGIN

from an hourly rate to a fixed fee, or a percentage of the total project cost—usually about 10 percent for small jobs and between 7 and 10 percent for larger projects. Check out the American Institute of Architects, www.aiaonline.com to find your local chapter, where you can find names of licensed architects in your area.

- **GENERAL CONTRACTOR:** Most jobs require a contractor to oversee the project. (A homeowner can be his or her own contractor, but this takes a lot of time and effort.) The contractor will execute the plans drawn up by the architect. A professional contractor should be familiar with local building codes and will be able to procure all necessary permits—in fact, this task should be included in your contract. Contractors also hire and supervise all tradespeople—called subcontractors or "subs"—involved in the project (tile setters, electricians, plumbers, etc.) and coordinate work schedules and procedures.

  Contractors' fees come in three different forms. Make sure you know how the contractor is charging you before you accept a bid. Some work on a "cost-plus" basis where the contractor charges a fee for his or her services plus the cost of the project (materials, services of subcontractors, etc.). Others have a fixed fee—the best option, since you know ahead of time what to expect. Still others work on a percentage of the total cost. If your contractor works on a percentage, make sure you keep track of expenses throughout the project, and ask your contractor for a cost breakdown. To find a contractor or a remodeler, visit the National Association of the Remodeling Industry's web site at www.nari.org.

A thirty-two-foot-high cathedral ceiling and heart-pine floor planks of different widths make this great room appear larger than it actually is. White walls set the stage for a fuss-free décor. White matelasse was used on the sofas and cotton duck slipcovers on the dining room chairs. The white palette is repeated in all the rooms for a unified look throughout the house.

ABOVE: This Napa Valley home features windows on both sides of a dramatic entry, offering stunning north and south views of the surrounding vineyards. Installing multiple banks of doors is an excellent way to bring natural light into a house.

OPPOSITE: Improved solar power and tax rebates have helped to encourage building environmentally responsible homes. As part of a remodel, the architect incorporated photovoltaic panels for solar power in this environmentally friendly home located in San Francisco.

BEFORE YOU BEGIN

- **CERTIFIED KITCHEN OR CERTIFIED BATH DESIGNER:** If you want a state-of-the-art kitchen or a luxurious bath, consider hiring a Certified Kitchen Designer (CKD) or Certified Bath Designer (CBD). These pros attend trade shows and conferences to keep up-to-date on the latest products, materials, and technology, as well as on building and safety codes. If you work with a CKD or CBD, you can expect a detailed outline of your project describing every element to be included, from wiring and plumbing to appliances and fixtures to counters, floors, and cabinets. For these pros, comfort, safety, and aesthetics are equal considerations in the success of your kitchen and bath. Take a look at the National Kitchen & Bath Association web site (www.nkba.com) for more information. Fees differ depending on the region and the scope of the project.

Salvaged architectural pieces and new millwork make a pleasing blend in the sunny open-plan kitchen. The lighting fixture above the island was adapted from an old pot rack.

TOP RIGHT: This home features a spacious kitchen with a generous breakfast area. Many homeowners opt to forgo a formal dining room in favor of a large breakfast area, preferring the casual atmosphere of dining in the kitchen.

BOTTOM RIGHT: Set in the heart of the floor plan, this kitchen enjoys the spotlight and is open to the living area. Granite covers both the counter-top and the backsplash around the cooktop.

BELOW: Although it looks old, the farmhouse sink is brand-new. Two deep basins make cleanup a snap, and the faucet is set high enough for large pots to fit underneath it.

ABOVE: Dual sinks and an oversized mirror smooth the morning rush hour for both husband and wife. The colors—tones of beige, cream, and white—are an extension of the same colors used in the master bedroom.

RIGHT: The designer of this breakfast nook decided to forego chairs in favor of an upholstered window bench. A hidden advantage: storage space lines the bottom of the unit below the cushion.

Narrowing the Field

Once you determine what type of expert you need, collect a list of names from family and friends. Then, conduct a preliminary interview on the phone to determine if this person will be right for you and your project. Next, meet with the pro in person. During this meeting, review their portfolio and try to get a feel for what their style is—and if it suits your needs. Finally, get at least two references and consult them. Ask the references what they liked and disliked about the particular professional. Also find out if they would use that person again. That is always a true test of whether the person really enjoyed the experience or not.

Tones of blue and green offer bursts of color into the otherwise neutral family room. Two-hundred thousand dollars was allotted for furnishing the 3,921 square feet of interior space in this model home.

- **INTERIOR DESIGNER:** An interior designer can play an important role in your project, from helping you select colors and furnishings to overseeing a team of professionals in a major remodel, but they are generally not qualified to plan any structural redesigns. Because interior designers have access to manufacturers that sell only to the trade, working with one can give you greater access to products and materials than you might have otherwise. Some interior designers charge an hourly fee for their services, while others apply a markup to products ordered. Most, however, combine these two options, charging an hourly rate and doubling the wholesale cost of goods. The American Society of Interior Designers will help you find a designer in your area; visit www.asid.org.

OPPOSITE: Mixing upholstered furnishings with unadorned wooden chairs provides an eclectic feel. The fireplace is carefully crafted to have an understated, refined elegance.

ABOVE LEFT: During the bidding process, check to see if the expert has included the manufacturers or a very detailed description of what you'll be getting. Here, for example, notice how the tiles extend up the wall.

ABOVE RIGHT: When working with your professionals, it's important to hammer out all the details ahead of time. In comparing bids, make sure they include details, such as how much and what kinds of fabric will be used.

The Bidding Process

Now that you've narrowed the field of candidates, you can start the bidding process. A bid is a formal, legally binding statement that a contractor will complete a job, described in detail in the document. (Note that an estimate is not the same as a bid. An estimate is not legally binding.) Get all your bids in writing on a standard form or the company's letterhead. Examine all the bids and compare and contrast what exactly you're getting. You might get a low bid from one contractor, but the materials may be lower quality. Be wary of very low bids; some contractors may be so desperate for the job that they offer a rock-bottom bid, but then cut corners to get the job done.

If you're working with an architect or interior designer, you can elect to be less involved in the selection and bidding process. You can allow your architect or designer to choose the contractor. In many cases this is advantageous, because the two have a good working relationship, and there is already

Here, architecture sets the tone of the living room. The linear ceiling treatment and the squared hearth create a restrained backdrop for traditional furniture shapes.

a level of trust established. However, watch out for a team that's too buddy-buddy. You don't want your architect or designer giving his stamp of approval just because of a friendship.

Get It in Writing

Drawing up a contract is one of the most important pieces of the building process. It's important to get everything in writing, so there won't be any misunderstandings down the road. Following is a list of elements that you'll need to make your contract ironclad.

- **DATE OF AGREEMENT.** All contracts should be dated, so if and when revisions are made, you'll be able to know which contract is the most recent (and most accurate).

BEFORE YOU BEGIN

When you have a team of experts that are truly professionals, you're sure to get great results. A case in point is this beautifully outfitted living room. A perfect palette, interesting built-ins, and carefully chosen materials combine to create a room where you love to be.

- **CONTACT INFORMATION FOR ALL PARTIES INVOLVED.** This must include the homeowners, the contractor, the person who may be supervising the project on a daily basis, subcontractors, including plumbers, electricians, roofers, and painters. Make sure to include addresses, phone numbers, and emergency contact numbers. You should also request insurance certificates for the subcontractors.

BEFORE YOU BEGIN

- **CONTRACTOR'S LICENSE AND/OR REGISTRATION NUMBER.**

- **DESCRIPTION OF THE WORK.** If drawings and plans will be included (see item below), the description of the work can be short and simple. Otherwise, it should describe the project in detail, and to avoid making the contract unwieldy, the description can be included as an appendix.

- **COPIES OF ALL DRAWINGS, PLANS, AND SPECIFICATIONS.** These items can also be made part of the appendix. Study plans carefully before you approve them, and make sure the contract stipulates that you must sign off on the plans before work begins.

- **DETAILED LIST OF ALL MATERIALS.** Be certain to include brand names, model numbers, colors, and descriptions of anything going into the house, appliances, fixtures, fittings, insulation, drywall, and the like. You should even specify the details down to the cabinet hardware and electrical switch plates—if those things are important to you. Otherwise, the contractor may select items that may not appeal to you aesthetically or not be up to your standards of quality. Beware of contracts that include the wording "or equivalent" following a specific model number. This wording can be risky, because it gives your contractor permission to determine what an equiv-

OPPOSITE: When planning a room, choose a natural focal point. For example, the hearth shown provides an anchor for the chairs and sofa around it.

BELOW: The arch over the fireplace in this family room echoes the arched doorways throughout the house. The 20 x 22-foot room includes a custom-coffered ceiling made of painted poplar.

alent is and to perhaps select the second choice instead of making efforts to find the first. A better solution is to insert a substitution of materials clause, which will state that your contractor may not substitute any materials or appliances without your written consent.

Also, specify which items are to be supplied by the homeowner and which are to be purchased by the contractor. This area of your contract should really spell out every material that you want in the house.

- **LIST OF SUPPLIERS.** A list of the names, business addresses, and phone numbers of all suppliers who will be sending materials to the site will be useful for determining who will be issuing lien releases (see page 27).

- **TOTAL CONTRACT AMOUNT, OR FINAL PRICE OF THE JOB.**

- **PAYMENT SCHEDULE.** A breakdown of the total amount due, stating the size and due date for each payment.

- **FINANCING CONTINGENCY.** Insert a clause that the contract is void if you fail to obtain financing at a rate you can afford by contract-signing time.

- **ASSIGNMENT OF RESPONSIBILITY** to the contractor for obtaining the necessary building permits, inspection approvals, and complying with zoning and building laws. It's best to leave this responsibility to your contractor rather than doing it yourself, because your contractor will be more familiar with the process—and will in turn be liable if the work does not comply with the local codes.

The contract should also include the price of permits, whether paid as a part of the contract price or as a purchase allowance, sometimes used when the price of the permit remains to be established. If you're using a purchase allowance, stipulate that the contractor provide original receipts on a building department invoice form or letterhead.

A 100-year-old Victorian house is updated with modern features. Two overhangs give the exterior of the Marblehead, Massachusetts cottage a quirky, but welcoming charm.

BEFORE YOU BEGIN

- **OWNER'S RIGHT OF SUPERVISION AND INSPECTION.** This important clause establishes that the work in progress must meet your approval and be subject to your inspection. It may appear to be in conflict with a standard, preprinted contract, which establishes the contractor's control over the job, but this amendment allows you to express your opinions or concerns about the project.

- **COMPLETION DATES.** Include a clause that sets a date for substantial completion (the time at which the project is usable and only minor work remains). Establish penalties for failure to complete on time, usually a deduction per day. Note: the contractor may want a bonus for finishing ahead of schedule.

ABOVE: An 8 x 8-foot painting takes center stage above the furniture grouping. Black slate floors provide a nice contrast to the stark white walls.

RIGHT: Like the architecture, the furnishings in the living room feature simple, modern lines. The daybed and chairs by Mies van der Rohe are classics.

- **PROJECT SCHEDULE.** You and your contractor should work out a schedule, so that you'll know what is expected to happen. It's crucial to include a commencement date and a finish date. Otherwise you may have the contractor taking other jobs while doing yours.

- **DAILY STARTING AND QUITTING TIMES** and hours during which the workers have access to the site.

- **CLEANUP POLICY.** You'll want to specify that each day dirt and debris should be removed, and tools and materials should be stored out of the way as safely and neatly as possible. At the end of the project, specify that you want the job site left "broom swept."

- **TYPE, AMOUNTS, AND POLICY NUMBERS OF ALL INSURANCE POLICIES** held by homeowner and contractor. This will ensure that each party knows about coverage.

ABOVE: With a team of experts, including an architect, interior designer, and builder, the homeowners reworked the layout of this house, made space for artwork, and created spaces that are comfortable.

OPPOSITE TOP: An avocado-colored wall sets the tone—literally—for this bath. A pedestal sink offers an elegant, updated touch.

OPPOSITE BOTTOM: A den doubles as a second bedroom when guests come. A photo of the white sands of New Mexico complements the black-and-white scheme.

- **Dispute resolution clause.** A contract should always include a provision for dispute settlement. It will state that if you and your contractor cannot come to an agreement amicably, your dispute will first go to mediation, then to binding arbitration with the service named in the contract.

- **Cancellation, or breach-of-contract clause.** In the event of poor workmanship or inability or refusal to meet the contract requirements, the homeowner must have the right to cancel.

- **Waiver of mechanics' liens.** This requires the contractor to provide you with proof (or lien release) at major stages of completion that subcontractors and suppliers have been paid.

- **Warranties.** This important provision should be carefully detailed, stating what it covers—labor, materials, or both—and for what length of time.

- **Change orders.** Include a statement that the homeowner has the right to make changes to the project after the contract has been signed. Each change should be accompanied by a mini-contract of its own with the specific details in writing and signed and dated by both parties.

- **Surplus materials.** In this clause, specify whether you want to keep any materials or equipment.

- **Final payment.** Make certain your contract spells out that you will not make a final payment until the job is completed to your satisfaction in every detail, and to the satisfaction of the appropriate local authorities. You must thoroughly inspect the entire project and have final release of lien, in writing, in your possession before you write that final check.

CHAPTER TWO

First Impressions

Architectural Styles

Today's homes cannot be categorized into one specific style or another. Often an architect or builder merges different characteristics from a variety of periods. To determine what you like, you must first learn the basic house styles. From traditional homes to contemporary structures, the choices are as diverse as they are beautiful.

- **EUROPEAN STYLE:** This category includes a broad range of homes, from French Country châteaux to Italian Mediterranean-style buildings. One of the earliest styles, dating from the 1400s, is the English Tudor. Tudors offer a sense of warmth with a design focused around a fireplace, timber frames, and arched doorways. In sixteenth-century Britain, the Tudor style marked a significant period in architecture; houses were moving away from the cold medieval castle to a place that felt more like a home. The English Manor and French Country home also afford a welcoming feeling with stone and brick exteriors, well-placed windows flanked by painted shutters, and plenty of charm. On the other side of the design spectrum is a Mediterranean-style home—one that features varied rooflines, turrets, and plenty of windows—and an overall open and airy quality that differs from Tudors and Manor homes.

Located in California, this Tuscan-style home offers a host of options, from a home office and nanny quarters to a junior master bedroom and additional garage space for a golf cart.

LEFT: When this 200-year-old Nantucket house was updated, the owner-architect stayed faithful to its old-time charm and character by choosing the same window and door trim, windows that closely match the originals, and white-cedar shingle siding, which quickly weathered to match the old shingles.

BELOW: Nestled on a pristine Alabama hillside, this compact cabin sits in harmony with its surroundings. While the exterior has a gently weathered look, the interior is completely contemporary.

- COLONIAL: When one thinks of a Colonial home, a grand, all-American traditional structure comes to mind. This classic-style home, originating in the early seventeenth-century after the settlers came to the New World and developed the Colonies, is generally built of wood or brick. Typical features include a stately entrance hall, plenty of architectural detail—such as moldings, wainscoting, and pediments above doorways—and a palette of subtle earth tones. Colonial style can be divided by region in that Southern Colonials have pitched roofs and dormers as well as a staircase located in the back of the house, while a New England Colonial might have Tudor and Elizabethan features and overhanging rooflines. The saltbox house evolved from the New England–style Colonial. The ubiquitous center-hall Colonial, first owned by wealthy merchants in the eighteenth century, features a symmetrical plan with rooms surrounding a staircase. This stately design offers a traditional look that transcends time and will never go out of style.

This Queen Anne–style home features a steeply pitched slate roof, and a mix of brick, clapboard, and shingle siding. The architect incorporated classic elements of the style for the exterior, such as cross gables, turrets, half-timber detailing, corbelled chimneys, and a sweeping veranda along the waterfront side of the house.

• **VICTORIAN:** The history of this house design is divided into British Victorian (1837–1901) and American Victorian (1840–1910), however, there are a number of styles and secondary movements that are now under the heading of "Victorian." For example, clean-looking Shingle-style houses with round towers as well as the highly decorative Queen Anne–style homes with patterned masonry and an abundance of millwork fall into this category.

• **CRAFTSMAN:** The Arts and Crafts movement, which lasted from 1860 to 1925, included many of the most influential designers of modern-day architecture. The strong horizontal designs from Frank Lloyd Wright, the beautiful interiors by William Morris and furnishings by Gustav Stickly, the unique exteriors by architect Sir Edwin Lutyens, as well as the fine craftsmanship of California builders Charles and Henry Greene, were just a few features representative of the period. What's typical of a Craftsman-style house? Intricate joinery, rooms of generous size, which today are our great rooms, casement windows, and detailed interiors, including decorated ceilings—with either plaster relief, wood beams, or stencils—and built-in furnishings.

• MODERN: Today's Modern homes are quite diverse. The architectural interest comes from the structural feats and innovative uses for new as well as old materials. Frank Lloyd Wright, for example, gave us a contemporary style in the 1930s with his cantilevered planes, while architect Frank Gehry shows us an organic form in his masterpiece in Bilbao, Spain. Albeit a commercial space, Spain's Guggenheim museum has made waves, no pun intended, in the architectural community and is sure to influence residential design in the future.

Modeled after the century old cabins in the area, this vacation home was designed to recede into its wooded surroundings and to take advantage of the landscape. Natural materials like cedar shingles, a stone foundation and chimney, and copper roofing on the turret help the house blend in gracefully with its lakeside setting.

ABOVE: This majestic house sits high on a bluff above the Hudson River and blends seamlessly into the landscape. Formal elements such as pillars, towers, and Palladian windows are softened by the natural shingles and dark green trim.

RIGHT: Three sets of French doors and a screened-in porch comprise the back of this 5,500-square-foot house in Westhampton, New York. A steeply pitched roofline, dormer windows, and new brick designed to look aged give the house a traditional look.

FIRST IMPRESSIONS

LEFT: "I have a passion for the spirit of the house," says the owner of the 1960s Phoenix ranch. The structure needed some updating, but the strong design remained. Every room in the house has a view of the mountains.

ABOVE: Defying categorization, this eclectic, Craft-inspired house utilizes the owners' collection of salvaged architectural objects, including collections of antique tiles, rescued stained glass, iron grillework, the front door of the house, and the brackets under the porch ceiling.

Exterior Treatments

The look of your house is partially determined by the exterior treatment you choose. Moreover, exterior siding preserves and protects your home from the elements. The variety of siding choices is extensive, but the one you choose will depend on regional influences, climate, and personal preferences as well as the particular demands of the home plan. Generally, siding options are interchangeable, though some work better in specific areas of the country and with certain weather conditions. Combining materials allows you to gain a rich, impressive look while potentially lowering the cost.

Quality should be a primary concern when shopping for siding. Since durability and longevity are directly related to cost, you'll want to install the best you can afford. You'll recoup the initial outlay in lower maintenance and replacement costs over the years. Here is an overview of the many options available on the market.

White-washed brick offers a soft, quiet appearance to a home. Here, the taupe shutters, garage door, and cedar shake roof complement the color of the brick.

- **WOOD:** One of the most popular choices, wood comes in traditional bevel or lap siding, horizontal cedar siding, and cedar shake shingles. Because real wood expands and contracts with the weather, this material can require extensive maintenance and must be repainted or stained periodically. Cedar and redwood are easier to maintain than softwoods, such as spruce and pine.

    Manufactured products—wood-composite clapboards, oriented strand board (OSB), and fiber-cement lap siding—offer the look and feel of real wood without the high maintenance. Generally, these products are more affordable than natural looks. Paneled shingles that match the look of cedar shingles are also an option. These attach to exterior walls quickly and easily, making them less expensive to install than true cedar shingles.

Cedar siding and stone marry the house to its rugged mountain setting. The builder also turned the clapboard rough-side out to absorb more stain.

- **BRICK:** According to the *Residential Cost Handbook* (a reference book for real estate appraisers), brick homes enjoy an appreciation on average that is 6 percent greater than identical homes with vinyl, wood, or aluminum siding. Known for its ability to withstand the elements and its resistance to decay and insects, brick is one of the more durable siding options. Brick is also easy to care for, a good insulator, and fire-resistant.

- **VINYL:** Among the more popular manufactured products, this low-cost option is not only easy to maintain, but also relatively easy to install. The thickness, or gauge, is the most important factor in durability and cost—the thicker, the better. Vinyl siding is available in a range of hues. Since the color permeates the material, the panels never need repainting or staining. A periodic washing keeps it looking its best. The negatives? Darker colors tend to fade, and the siding can melt and burn.

ABOVE LEFT: Get the look of stucco without the hassle and expense. Here, bricks are made to look as if they have a stucco finish.

ABOVE RIGHT: The brick seen on most new houses today is not a structural component, but rather a veneer on wood framing. Brick lends a distinctly classic, handcrafted look to a home.

This storybook charmer gets its good looks from the exterior of unevenly-sized stones. That, along with scaled-down windows and wood shutters, makes this house a home.

- **ALUMINUM AND STEEL:** Like vinyl, aluminum and steel sidings are also very sturdy, easy-care products. Though they can be dented and the lower gauge versions may bend or warp, metal sidings are fire-, rot-, and bug-resistant. These products also benefit from occasional washing, and may need to be repainted. Some brands of both aluminum and steel siding are coated with polyvinyl chloride (PVC) finishes to protect them and make them easier to maintain.

- **STUCCO:** This long-lasting material is a combination of cement and sand that is applied with a trowel to concrete block or wood framing. Widely used as an all-over siding material for homes in warm climates, stucco is also a distinctive accent material for chimneys, garages, and foundations. Stucco is easy to maintain, but may need repainting over time. Now, companies are making products that look like stucco as well.

- **STONE:** Enduring with a unique, sometimes rustic, look, true stone façades can be very expensive. For a less costly alternative, consider using stone as a detail. Or investigate one of the synthetic stone products now available, which are lightweight, easy to install, and affordable.

Rooflines

Whether your roof is composed of shingles, shakes, clay tile, slate, or metal, the style of the roof has a big impact on the look of your home. When expressing what you like to your architect or builder, make sure to show him or her photos of the types of roof that appeal to you. Certain types are more appropriate to particular climates. For example, you cannot have a flat roof in a wet climate, because the roof must provide for the water runoff. Also, the style of a home often dictates the roofline. Mediterranean-style houses, for instance, generally feature Spanish-style roofs, whereas Victorian structures often have mansard roofs—each side gently steps down in its pitch, creating a distinct shape. Most likely, your designer will have a roof structure in mind, but you may want to add features like dormers to get extra space and add architectural interest. There are a few different types: Gable dormers have a pitched roof, while shed dormers feature a flat roof, and an eyebrow is a type of low dormer with a curved, not surprisingly, eyebrow shape.

You'll want your home to make a good first impression. Here, a brick path with ample plantings and lighting makes guests feel welcome immediately. The swinging gate is a nostalgic touch and signals that there is more to discover beyond the fence.

Going Green

Green design, also known as environmentally-conscious building, is a popular topic in environmental, architectural, and landscaping circles. But this topic is not only for the professionals. It's easy for you as a consumer to educate yourself on the benefits of green design, and it may also help in cutting costs. If done correctly, green design is low-maintenance, cost-effective, and environmentally responsible.

- **BUILD WISELY.** Building a new home? Talk with your architect about construction alternatives. There are several green techniques, but two popular types are rammed earth and straw bale construction. In rammed earth construction, a mixture of soil, water, and concrete is made and then this moist substance is pounded into sturdy blocks that are then used to build. This method uses inexpensive materials with high energy efficiency. In

Green design emphasizes the use of native plants which will thrive on their own accord. You'll save water and add beauty to your backyard.

straw bale construction, the bales are compressed and tied together and then covered with plaster or stucco coating. This method is cost-effective, energy efficient, and has a low environmental impact.

- **CHOOSE THE RIGHT MATERIALS.** A few years ago, our choices for environmental building products were limited. Today, that's not the case. Environmentally concerned companies have begun developing and producing these materials in a variety of styles. You can build your home from the foundation to the roof, from the interior to the exterior, with green materials. Also, check with your contractor about using recycled products during construction. This is another way to help the environment and save money in the process.

- **SAVE ENERGY.** The typical home loses more than 25 percent of its heat through windows, so total window area should not exceed 8 to 9 percent of the floor area, unless passive solar techniques are used. Select windows that have high insulation R-values (the measurement of its resistance to heat flow), and low-E (low emittance) glass with solar-control coatings and insulated frames. For windows and appliances, look for the Energy Star label which ensures that the product has gone through a certain level of testing for energy efficiency. You can also do things like turn down the setting on your water heater, and thoroughly insulate your home.

- **LANDSCAPE EFFECTIVELY.** Whether you're building a new home or enhancing an existing house, there are many ways to landscape with energy conservation in mind. For example, plant windbreaks, such as evergreen trees, on the north side of your house and plant deciduous trees on the south and west corners to provide shade in the summer and sun in the winter. To conserve water choose plants like those native to the area that require less water. Also, install an irrigation system that uses significantly less water than a sprinkler and consider alternatives to lawns, which

Today's vinyl windows offer durability and insulating value, plus enough style and dramatic impact for the most high-end projects.

require more water than any other part of your landscape. In addition, you can recycle yard scraps and grass cuttings into mulch and place it around your plants to help retain moisture and reduce weeds. Using your own mulch saves money and maintenance—and helps the environment by keeping this yard debris from ending up in a landfill.

Remember that sustainable design is a relatively new concept. Although there are many more companies today who offer green products than there were even a year ago, you still need to give yourself plenty of time to research products. And take the time to find a professional who really is an advocate of green building. Keep in mind, too, that some of these methods may cost more initially, but the long-term savings can be substantial.

Thanks to improving technology, today's double-hung windows pair classic looks with energy efficiency and easy operation.

Adding Curb Appeal

Landscaping not only enhances the environment, but it also may increase the value of your property at resale. By adding plantings, ground cover, trees, and ornamental shrubs, you will add curb appeal to your home. Imagine driving up to a house that had beautiful flowering plants lining the front steps and trees framing the structure. This would make a good first impression before even entering the home. What door you select, even the door handle, steps, overhangs, or trellises—all will make a statement and add curb appeal. And don't forget lighting. Exterior lighting will certainly enhance your home as well as provide a safe environment. Professional landscape designers can devise a lighting plan—or there are products, which are low-voltage, that you can install yourself. Real estate agents agree, giving your home curb appeal is a surefire way to help in selling the house—and more than likely it will increase the home's value.

CHAPTER THREE

Grand Entrances

Great Shapes

First impressions are very important. Your entryway will set the tone for the rest of your interior. Therefore, when reviewing floor plans, examine the entry space with as much thought as you would, say, your master suite. To help you define your preferences for your entryway, consider the following list of questions. Your answers should help guide you to the type of space you want.

- **DO YOU WANT A HALLWAY LEADING INTO YOUR LIVING SPACE?** This idea can be very dramatic. Perhaps you walk into a modestly scaled hallway with a standard 8-foot ceiling—which leads to an open, double-height great room.

- **ARE YOU DRAWN TO CHARMING ENTRIES?** If so, start by considering the shape, the number and size of the windows, and the architectural details in the room. To create an intimate space, consider a square or rectangular shape for the room. And if you're looking for charm, you'll certainly want something modest in scale, rather than a room that's overwhelming. Think about your decorative touches—maybe an antique lantern overhead, plenty of moldings and a rich color. You may even want to include stained glass panes to provide visual interest. When light enters, an array of colors will bounce off the walls, floors and ceiling.

Framed by stately original molding, glass doors open from the entry hall into the living room where fine furnishings have been carefully arranged around the fireplace.

Salvaged architectural elements set the tone inside this home, beginning with the entryway where the magnificent stained glass window in the entry was rescued from a demolished house in Pennsylvania. The light fixture is another salvaged piece, this time from an old church.

- **HOW ABOUT A CIRCULAR VESTIBULE?** Another dramatic choice, a rounded space often creates a serene atmosphere. Furniture placement is a bit trickier when you're working with curves. In a round room, niches built into the walls can display favorite collectibles or artwork. Whether you've planned for a square, rectangle, circle, or even an octagon for your entry shape, consider the additional questions below.

- **WHAT KINDS OF FURNISHINGS WILL YOU INCLUDE?** How large are the pieces? If you have a family treasure that you know you want to include in your entry, make sure there is a spot for it in your floor plan. Will you include an area rug in this space?

- **DO YOU WANT STORAGE IN THIS SPACE?** Check your plan to see if there is a closet slated for the entry. If you live in an area with cold winters, a spot to hold those bulky coats, scarves, and hats will be your first consideration. Your second? A seat where people can remove their snowy boots!

- **HOW WILL YOU LIGHT THE SPACE?** Are there windows in the space? Is there a skylight? If so, this may provide enough daylight, but you will need artificial light in the evening. Do you want one hanging pendant light or a large chandelier when you first enter? Perhaps the soft glow of wall sconces or lights set over pieces of art will give all the illumination the room needs. You may also desire simple recessed lights, and for those with modern spaces who prefer to keep the décor spare, consider lighting that makes no statement at all.

- **WHAT ABOUT ANY SPECIAL NEEDS?** Do you have any elderly people living in the home? Do you need wide spaces and doorways to accommodate wheelchairs? Do you need a ramped entry? Consult with your architect or builder to make sure he or she knows how to design the space to code.

Architectural Features

The design of the foyer should relate to the adjacent rooms. Architectural features help to either delineate the individual zones—especially in an open-plan design—or add continuity from one space to another. Following are features that will take your design from fine to fabulous.

- **COLUMNS:** In some cases, columns can be structural. However, columns are usually included to provide visual interest and make a statement. If you have an open entryway, you may want to add two columns (or even four) to create definition between your entrance and living area. Take a look at your old high school history books to see what kind of column you like. Generally composed of a base, shaft, and a capital, columns are most commonly seen in the three Ancient Greek styles. Doric is the earliest and

simplest-looking of the Classical Orders; Ionic, a column with the curving volutes at the top; and Corinthian, the most ornate of the three, includes elaborately detailed acanthus leaves.

- **ARCHWAYS:** An archway affords a graceful entrance to any space. Talk to your architect or designer about how you envision the arch. Ask him or her to draw an elevation (a two-dimensional architectural drawing, done to scale) of the space, so that you can see the curve of the arch, its framing, and any moldings that will adorn it.

- **TRANSOM LIGHTS:** If you have a rectangular entry, you might consider installing a transom window above it. A transom is a pane of glass, or a series of panes that is hinged from the top or bottom of the sash. The feature not only adds architectural interest, but it also allows light to pass from one space to another. Transoms can also be found over the entry door.

- **STEPS:** Don't overlook your vertical spaces. By adding levels, you instantly create zones. Even a single step up or down will delineate an entry from the living area. Or if your plan allows, you might add a few steps for drama. Think about how you want these steps designed. Stairs with low risers and broad treads are gracious in any architectural style, and they are the easiest to climb. Think about the building material for the steps and the design of the rail or the banister. Would you like to line them with carpet or a runner? It's also extremely important to make sure that the stepped area is incorporated in such a way that visitors don't trip going into your living spaces.

- **MOLDINGS:** Moldings are a great way to add architectural detail. Installing molding can be very affordable, especially if you do it yourself. Again, you can use this feature to either delineate certain areas by using different types of moldings—or molding in one area and not another—or to keep a continuous look throughout the home by running the same type of molding throughout. Also, consider decorative features like bead-board, paneling, and chair rails. These all can add charm and distinction to entries. Choices for moldings today have never been so diverse. Not only must you select the style, but you must also decide on the material. Moldings come in wood and lightweight polyurethane. Wood is very affordable, but the polyurethane may be easier to install and does not warp with time.

RIGHT: These linoleum tiles are made from organic materials that are naturally antistatic and antibacterial, making them ideal for high-traffic areas like the foyer. They're also a cinch to mop clean.

BELOW: Floor medallions make a beautiful statement in an entry. This one was created from several species of reclaimed wood.

Flooring

What do you imagine underfoot in your entryway? Do you want to be greeted with marble or a large, inlaid medallion? Wood and tile floor manufacturers are now making medallion products that don't require as much labor as those available in the past, and in turn these units are more affordable. This is true of mosaic tile borders as well. Mosaics are now delivered on a piece of mesh, so that they can be installed on your floor without much labor, other than grouting the material.

On a practical note, select a material that is appropriate for an entryway. With constant traffic, you'll need a floor that wears well. Ceramic tile, for example, is an excellent choice. It's durable and easy to keep clean. Wood and laminate floors will also stand the test of time.

OPPOSITE: The main stairway and a pair of columns in lieu of a wall create an open space. Tucked against the stair are a desk and a bookcase behind it—a great spot for taking care of those to-do lists.

RIGHT: Some of your crucial decisions will be about surfacing. Have a firm idea of your needs and wants before you begin shopping, and be sure to consider maintenance. The coffered ceiling in this living room adds an extra element of grandeur to the sweeping staircase.

Staircases

Depending on your plan, your staircase may be the focal point of your entrance. You must decide if you want to make the stair really stand out in your entrance. If so, would you like a sweeping stair, curving upwards to the second level of your home, a straight stair, a spiral stair, or a dramatic double stair? Obviously, a double stair will take up considerable more room than a straight stair. Certain types of houses are more appropriate for certain stair styles. For example, if you're building a contemporary structure, you may want to consider a metal spiral stair, whereas a wood stair is generally selected for a front hall Colonial.

When you think about the design of your stair, you'll need to know some general terms:

- **TREAD:** The portion of the step you place your foot on.

- **RISER:** The vertical part of the step.

- **STRINGS:** The sides of the stairway, which anchor the steps.

- **NEWEL POST:** The larger vertical supports that mark the beginning and end of the stairway. There are also half newels, which are smaller posts that generally mark a turning point for the stair.

- **BALUSTERS:** The smaller vertical posts that run between the newel posts.

- **BALUSTRADE:** This term refers to the whole railing, consisting of the newel posts, balusters, and handrail.

- **POST-TO-POST DESIGN:** When a handrail is set lower than the height of the newel post.

- **OVER-THE-POST DESIGN:** When the handrail sits atop the newel post and creates a continuous effect.

There are so many choices to make in deciding upon a design for your staircase. In fact, there are entire books on the subject. To start, examine the design of your home. What type of stair will look best and will fit with your floor plan? Your architect or builder can guide you. If you want a modern staircase, you still have plenty of options. Consider building a half-wall in lieu of balusters, for example. A half-wall gives the stair a clean look. Metal stairs also impart contemporary flair. Materials like galvanized steel and glass are good choices for a sleek aesthetic. If your home has a traditional style, look for such details as returned treads, where the platform of the step extends slightly over the side.

Think about your railing. How do you want to finish off the newel posts? Do you want a square cap or perhaps a shape that's more organic? And there are a wide variety of post designs. From simple spindles to ornate wrought-iron shapes, the railing will play a big part in setting the tone for the stair.

Finally, consider what kind of storage space you'd like beneath the stair. Do you have room to fit a coat closet, which might come in handy in an entrance? You and your architect should decide whether to make the first step bigger than the others to create a welcoming effect.

Honey-toned wood floors topped by a simple runner keep this entry clutter-free. These unassuming materials welcome friends, family, and even pets.

OPPOSITE: A simple staircase provides function without blocking the view of the massive stone fireplace, which is the focal point of the living room.

ABOVE: At the top of the stair is a view of the gas fireplace which is suspended in the hallway wall. Because there are so many unique elements in the home, the stair has a minimalist design.

ABOVE: Artfully crafted, a cushioned bench sits neatly against the stairwell. A series of stained glass windows allows light to wash the space with an array of colors.

OPPOSITE: The winding staircase features iron balusters topped by a mahogany handrail. Carpet in a handsome pattern finishes off the distinctive stair. A marble medallion also adds interest in the entryway.

GRAND ENTRANCES

CHAPTER FOUR

Living Spaces

Open-Plan Design

Over the last few decades there has been a strong trend toward open-plan designs where the kitchen opens to a great room. Today, almost every new house includes some variation on this setup. An open plan gives a home a living space that feels larger than one that is enclosed by walls and doors. It also allows the cook in the family to be a part of the conversation; he or she is no longer isolated in the kitchen preparing a meal. The benefits of an open-plan design strongly outweigh the negatives.

What are the negatives? An open-plan design offers a more informal, casual feeling which some people dislike. In certain cases the great room encompasses a dining space, and there is not room for a formal dining area. Also, with this scheme you need to think about how to handle noise, since there are no walls to act as barriers and no doors to shut.

Trusses, latticework, and slatted windows create a sense of a sheltering tree canopy in this sophisticated cabin in the hills of Alabama. The soaring ceiling reaches twenty-five feet at its peak.

LEFT: Moldings and columns add architectural character to this 24 x 26-foot great room flanked by a dining room and kitchen on one side and a master suite on the other. To create a spacious feeling in the main living areas, the ceilings throughout the first floor are nine-feet high, and French doors were installed along the south-facing, rear façade.

OPPOSITE, TOP: Furniture found at flea markets mix with upscale pieces in the living room of this town house. Every effort was made to imbue the home with energy-saving features, such as windows with a low-emittance coating that reduces the heat loss.

OPPOSITE, BOTTOM: An elegant corner in this open-plan home features a gas fireplace and comfortable chair. Spare and elegant, the living area is filled with natural light and has hardwood floors in a rich, dark color.

However, the majority of homeowners like having a large open space with easy access to the kitchen. It certainly seems like a trend that is going to stay for years to come.

Activity Zones

With both traditional and open-plan designs, you need to decide on the relative sizes of the rooms. Do you want an enormous kitchen with a large island in the center? Or would you prefer a compact kitchen to create more room for your living areas? Consider the relationships of your activity zones—living, dining, and cooking.

Your architect or designer will give you a scheme that he or she thinks best. However, adjustments can be made. Think about whether you want your main eating area to be right in the middle of the kitchen or set off in a corner of the room. You'll also need to create seating areas. Study how your living space will relate to the kitchen area. Is there a fireplace in the design? If so, more than likely, you'll want to have seating around that—so, figure out if the location of the fireplace is conducive to socializing as well as how it relates to the kitchen area. Do you want your company to be facing the kitchen while they're in the living area, or do you prefer to separate the zones a bit?

Talk with your professional about how you'd like to use the great room area. Do you need a quiet place for reading? Or a spot for paying bills?

Perhaps a writing desk will be incorporated in the design.

In a traditional plan, the spaces are defined by the walls, so you don't have to worry about the surrounding noise. In this scenario, you'll want to consider the flow of the spaces. How will the cook bring meals to the dining area? Is there easy access? In many homes that feature a traditional plan, there is a formal living room and then there's a family room or den. Check the floor plan to ensure that you like the size of the rooms. Do you want a larger family room and a smaller formal living area?

Notice, too, how spaces, either traditional or open-plan, relate to the entryway. What do you want guests to see immediately? Think about ceiling heights. To create drama, you could enter a small foyer with a low ceiling and then walk into a great room with a double-height ceiling. See how windows are placed throughout the plan. Do your living areas take advantage of the views? Obviously, when there's an obstructed view on one side of your house, you'll want to place, say, a powder room or closet on that wall, rather than large windows or your main living area. Try to envision yourself going through the house. There should be a natural flow from one area to another.

ABOVE: In this spacious home in the Rockies, the living room is situated to take advantage of the views. The ceiling is made of pine with Douglas fir beams, and the floor is slate. Overstuffed furniture softens the room's stone surfaces. An eighteen-inch-wide stone ledge under the windows provides additional seating.

OPPOSITE: The high, beamed ceiling gives a rustic feel to this comfortable family room. A media center occupies the far end of the fireplace wall, and the raised hearth runs the length of the wall.

LIVING SPACES

OPPOSITE: Although the great room looks too sophisticated for use by children, its easy-to-maintain features, such as hardwood floors, make it a family gathering spot. The custom-made banquette under the window is upholstered in a new faux leather that feels like leather but easily wipes clean.

ABOVE: With its classical crown molding the living room could seem a very formal place, but the soft colors, comfortable furniture, and ample sunlight give it a more casual atmosphere.

That's Entertainment

Today, most living areas include some kind of media system. It may just be a small TV, or it may be a full-fledged entertainment system. Either way, this needs advance planning, because the components you choose will affect your design.

- **TELEVISIONS:** Choices include rear-projection, front-projection, picture tube, and flat screens. With any of these, calculations and measurements must be done to figure out how much space you'll need in the room and how far away viewers should be—in addition to how the television will be displayed. For example, flat-screen TVs, which are available as plasma, LCD, and standard picture tube, feature a low profile which increases your options when it comes to interior design: You're no longer tied to the TV as a room's focal point. Flat TVs can be viewed from anywhere in the room without sacrificing the image quality, because the TV's surface appears bright and clear, especially from an angle. This may change how

At the heart of this home's open floor plan is the wide-open great room, which hosts every sort of activity, from watching TV to cocktails for a group of friends. The cabinets to the left of the fireplace provide storage. Similar cabinets on the other side of the fireplace hold the television and stereo equipment.

you design the space. Television sizes range from 10 inches to over 60 inches. (Note that the sizes are derived from taking a diagonal measurement of the screen.)

Whatever size television you select, the rule of thumb is that your viewing distance should be 1.5 times the screen width. So keep that calculation in mind when planning your seating area.

- **DVDs and Sound Systems:** It is important to know how many components you'll need to store, and where you will put all the speakers. Surround-sound systems generally include five speakers plus a subwoofer. There is a big range in speaker size. Now you can buy speakers that measure only a few inches and can be camouflaged into your design scheme. The subwoofer, however, might still require a special spot, as it is usually a larger unit.

Pine cabinetry storing a bar and entertainment center flanks the stone fireplace in this spacious living area that's part of an addition to a 200-year-old farmhouse. Dubbed the "club room" by the homeowners, it's located next to the kitchen and used frequently to entertain guests.

Storage and Display

With the trend of incorporating entertainment systems in the main living space, designers are faced with the challenge of creating an attractive environment with the equipment. The advent of sleek, flat-screen TVs has allowed designers and homeowners to hang the units on the wall, akin to a piece of artwork. Some people will even place a flat-screen TV over the fireplace, creating two focal points in the space. However, be wary that the temperature from the fireplace does not get too hot for the TV. If it rises above 90° F, the unit's life will be significantly shortened.

While some homeowners like the sleek look of their high-tech television system on display, others prefer a more traditional atmosphere for their living space. Luckily, cabinet manufacturers have accommodated this preference and have designed units that include furniture-like detailing to house the equipment. Features like turned legs, crown moldings, and corbels grace units to give the cabinetry Old-World style. You can even get handcrafted details, such as carvings or hand-painted embellishments, to enhance the charm of the storage unit. With the fine details of the cabinetry, the TV and various components are a bit less obvious.

To hide units completely, consider an armoire, where the television sits behind closed doors when not in use. Another clever trick to hide unattractive equipment is to hang curtains that can be drawn, or consider a screen that rolls up or neatly tucks into a wall or cabinet.

Floors, Walls and Ceilings

Before you install that big screen TV or theater-quality sound system, you'll need to select the materials for the shell of the living space. Here's a rundown of factors to consider when choosing walls, floors, and ceilings.

- **FLOORS:** If you do, in fact, plan to have a media system in your living area, talk to your designer about acoustics in the room; you may need a combination of sound-absorbing materials, like carpets, and sound-reflecting products, such has hardwood floors. Another consideration with regard to flooring: open plan versus traditional plan. With an open-plan design, you may need to be a bit more creative than you do with a traditional set of rooms, because the rooms have to complement one another. Either you can choose one type of flooring for the entire area, or a mixture of floors to define each zone. If you select

A prominent stone fireplace and diamond-light windows are classic features of shingle-style houses built at the turn of the twentieth century and are the inspiration behind this new home in New Hampshire. A cherry floor and cheerful colors create a welcoming ambiance.

one type of flooring for the entire area—living, dining, and kitchen—make sure it's suitable for all your needs. For example, carpet might be a great choice for the living areas, but you wouldn't want it in the kitchen with water, lots of spills, and high traffic. On the other hand, tile, which is a durable, low-maintenance choice and is especially practical in an eating area, is hard and cold, which may not appeal to you for your living space.

Finally, your home's location will be a factor in determining your flooring. If you reside in a warm climate, for instance, tile might be the perfect option for you, especially if your home is on or near the beach, as sand is easily swept from a tile floor. Also be wary of the way moisture affects your flooring if you live in a humid climate. Consult with your design expert to see what he or she recommends for your living space.

ABOVE: Soft underfoot, wall-to-wall carpet in a neutral-toned nylon adds warmth to this ski house in Windham, New York. Even the French doors and stock windows are specifically designed for the cold climate.

OPPOSITE: The great room is the center of this 5,400-square-foot home. Its thirty-foot-high and twelve-foot-wide fireplace was constructed of river stone. Exposed beams, vaulted ceilings, and pine floors give the room a rustic but sophisticated log-home look.

LIVING SPACES

LEFT: A dramatic dining room is graced with red walls and carpet and set behind carved doors from China, circa 1825. This room is a welcome change from the others in the house that feature more neutral tones.

BELOW: Queen Anne furniture, an oriental rug, and a traditional chandelier grace this beautifully appointed dining room. But it's the delicate blue walls, lined with white trim, that really add elegance.

- **WALLS:** Again, determine how you want the spaces to flow. Is your goal to keep a continuous look for the rooms? If so, select hues that complement one another. Stay with light tones for a calming effect. A good way to tell if colors will work well together is to look at a color wheel and select colors with the same amount of saturation. On the other hand, if your intention is to make more of a statement, say, in the dining area, choose a deep red to make that room really stand out.

    In terms of materials, the most common options for great walls are paint and wallcoverings. Paint is often the most affordable choice. Select different finishes for different rooms; flat paint is appropriate for living rooms,

This Vermont home's unique timber-frame construction is showcased in the one-and-a-half story living room. The walls are made of pine, which is easy to maintain and will become richer and darker with age. French doors and a bank of windows allow ample sunlight to pour in.

but in areas like the kitchen, choose a semigloss or high-gloss finish. The higher the gloss, the easier the paint will be to keep clean. There are also special kitchen paints that resist moisture to prevent mold from forming.

When choosing paint colors, start by bringing home paint chips. Try to get as many as possible. Once you narrow the choices, buy small containers of your favorites to see if you like them on your wall. Some brands now have small sized cans, intended for painting a small swatch on your walls. Paint a square measuring about 2 x 2 feet and examine it in all kinds of light to see if you like the color.

Faux-finishing is certainly not new, however, paint manufacturers today have made it easier for homeowners to create unique looks. Now paint companies offer special paints with instructions to achieve a certain effect. A suede and denim finish, for example, give a warm look to living spaces. And if you're not interested in a do-it-yourself project, consider wallpaper. Wallpapers mimicking a range of painted faux finishes are now available.

In addition, wallcoverings are available in different materials. For a retro look in your living space, consider a grasscloth wallcovering. In the kitchen, select wallcoverings that resist stains. Your retailer can tell you what's appropriate for a kitchen.

For the kitchen, you'll need to think about your backsplash. Here, your options include paint, tiles, solid surfacing, concrete, and stainless steel. Your counter material will determine what you'll use for your backsplash. For example, if you have selected a solid-surface counter, consider running it up the wall. When the counter and back wall blend smoothly, cleanup becomes a snap, because there is no joint to trap dirt.

ABOVE: This 3,221-square-foot town house is configured so that there are windows on three sides. The living area is open but formal and filled with light from an expansive wall of windows.

LEFT: Pale pastels work together for a pleasing effect in this house. A blush tone greets you and then a light blue affords a subtle backdrop for the fireplace in the living room.

LIVING SPACES

Character Builders

Installing moldings to walls adds instant character. Here are some common types and terms you should know when buying molding:

- **BASE:** Millwork that is adhered to the bottom of the wall.

- **CHAIR RAIL:** A horizontal molding mounted at chair height, and often used in conjunction with wainscoting to finish off the look.

- **CROWN MOLDING:** Angled molding, generally applied close to the ceiling to visually soften the connection between the ceiling and the wall.

- **DENTIL MOLDING:** A type of trim that resembles teeth.

- **EGG AND DART MOLDING:** A somewhat ornate design that alternates oval shapes and arrowheads.

- **CEILINGS:** Don't forget about the fifth wall. The ceiling can really make a statement in a home, whether you enhance it architecturally or decoratively. Discuss with your architect how the heights of the ceilings will change throughout the living areas, as it may not be obvious from the floor plan. In some cases ceilings are drawn with a dotted line on the plan. The style of your home sometimes dictates what the ceiling will look like. A Craftsman-style house may include wood beams on the ceiling, while a modern home might have plenty of double-height spaces.

  To make rooms appear taller, one trick is to paint the ceiling a lighter color than what's on the wall. Conversely, if you want to make a space feel cozy, use a stronger tone on the ceiling than what covers the walls.

  For the kitchen, consider adding charm by installing embossed metal ceiling tiles. You can also purchase wallpaper that looks like the old-fashioned tin ceilings, which is an easier material to install on your ceiling. A unusual ceiling will delight family members and be a conversation piece for guests.

The architecture really just frames the spectacular views from this Wyoming home. Warm wood-beamed ceilings, plenty of windows, and wood floors complement the mountain setting.

CHAPTER FIVE

Kitchens

Planning Your Kitchen

As you plan your new kitchen, you'll no doubt enjoy choosing the appliances, finishes, and storage features you've always coveted. But it's no less important—in fact it's absolutely essential—to consider the layout. To determine the best floor plan for your needs, think about how you will use the space. How large is it? How many people will be in the kitchen at a given time? Will more than one person cook? Clean up? Do you want the space to be inviting to guests? Do you hope to entertain there? Would you like to watch your kids do their homework at the breakfast table while you make dinner? All these factors and more determine the best shape for your work space. It's important to talk to your family and figure out how you'll be using the kitchen before you start installing your appliances.

Whether you love the look of light maple cabinets or favor dark-toned units like those shown here, stainless steel appliances work well with every decorating scheme.

Layout Basics

There are four basic layouts for a kitchen: galley, L-shape, U-shape, and G-shape. Each has its pro and cons, but all depend on the concept of the work triangle. A fundamental part of kitchen design for the last several decades, the work triangle describes the relationship among the three major kitchen work areas—the refrigerator, the cooktop and oven, and the sink. For the ultimate efficiency, the imaginary triangle connecting these three elements should conform to certain general standards developed by the National Kitchen & Bath Association (www.nkba.org). They are as follows:

An L-shaped kitchen creates an elongated work triangle, which the homeowner finds very efficient. Another favorite feature: The textured laminate finish on the cabinets don't show fingerprints.

With a large square island separating the work zone from a breakfast nook, the homeowners can easily prepare meals in the kitchen while family and friends take a seat in the adjacent area.

- Each triangle leg should measure between 4 and 9 feet long.

- The total length of all three legs should equal between 12 and 26 feet.

- General traffic patterns should not interfere with the work triangle.

- Cabinetry should not intersect any triangle leg by more than 12 inches.

ABOVE: A large island topped with butcher block is perfect for this baker. She can simply roll out the dough right on the counter. Candle chandeliers enhance the kitchen's overall elegance.

OPPOSITE: The owner wanted to give her kitchen a European flair. To get that look, she chose distressed cabinets surrounded by elaborate molding, including fluting, roping, and corbels.

Selecting Materials

With so many products on the market today, it's hard to figure out what materials to use in your kitchen. To find a style you like, flip through magazines and books and mark the pages featuring products you admire. Next, scour the Internet for information about the materials. The Internet can also give you a sense of what things cost. Finally, go to the stores and ask plenty of questions. You'll want to know the time required to install the product, whether it is in stock, how durable it is, and how to maintain it.

For counters, the options include the following:

- TILE: Tile comes in ceramic, porcelain, and stone. It's extremely durable, but if you select small tiles, the grout may become a nuisance to clean. However, if you love the look of a granite counter, but you're on a budget, consider buying granite tiles. These will be less expensive to install than a granite slab counter.

- LAMINATE: This synthetic material is an affordable option that comes in a range of colors. Laminate is made from layers of plastic, with the design or color on the top.

- SOLID SURFACING: Composed of acrylic or a blend of acrylic and polyester and made to look like stone, this product is extremely durable. Also, you can get an integrated sink made from solid

OPPOSITE, TOP: For a warm, natural look there's nothing like real wood counters. This counter has stainless steel rods adhered to the wood to create a built-in trivet to protect the wood from hot pots and pans.

OPPOSITE, BOTTOM: With quartz surfacing you can have a rounded edge on your counter. This strong, stain- and scratch-resistant material replicates the look of granite and is a great option for hard-working kitchens.

RIGHT: Granite countertops add just the right amount of glamour while taking all the wear and tear a family can dish out. A raised bar hides any mess on the counter, which the hosts appreciate when entertaining.

surfacing. When the sink and counter are one unit, there are no cracks in which dirt can hide.

- **QUARTZ SURFACING:** A relatively new category of counters has emerged. Pieces of quartz are incorporated into the counter to give it a bit of sparkle and visual depth.

KITCHENS

TOP: For the island, the designers chose white Corian counters with dual under-mounted stainless sinks. The island overlooks the living area as well as the dining nook off to the left.

ABOVE: Crafted of ceramic tile with a metallic gray finish and a metal accent strip, the backsplash provides a sheen to the otherwise neutral tones of the kitchen.

OPPOSITE: It's a simple combination, but it works: White counters, wood cabinets, and stainless steel appliances combine in a classic look that will never go out of style.

- **BUTCHER BLOCK:** This is especially popular for islands. If butcher block is near a sink, make sure it is sealed properly to protect against moisture. This product allows a homeowner to work right on the counter. Bakers love it.

- **CONCRETE:** A great option that offers a Zen-like quality to a kitchen. It can be infused with color and molded into almost any form. Although concrete itself is not costly, the installation makes this product a luxury item.

- **STONE:** Granite, marble, and soapstone are all popular options. Stone offers a natural look, but can be quite expensive.

- **METALS:** Stainless steel is now gracing counters and backsplashes. There are also lookalike materials that mimic metals.

Many of the same options for countertops exist for floors, such as tile, laminate, concrete, and stone. Vinyl and linoleum are also good choices for kitchens, due to their ease of maintenance. Wood floors, which always have been popular, are now seeing a revival, but with a twist—homeowners are looking for more exotic types of wood. According to the National Wood Flooring Association, "The thrill of the unknown and a taste for foreign lands have created an increase in the exotic wood flooring market." When you're dealing with a wood floor in the kitchen, it's crucial that it is sealed properly.

Caring for Hardwood Floors

Hardwood floors are among the easiest of flooring to care for. With little regular maintenance, they hold their beauty and performance for years.

- Sweep or vacuum regularly, to eliminate dirt and grit.

- Wipe spills promptly.

- Read and follow all manufacturer's care recommendations.

- Never wet mop—use only a slightly damp cloth and towel dry. Too much moisture can cause the wood to swell or buckle.

- Never use a self-polishing acrylic wax. It will make the wood dull and can only be removed by sanding and refinishing.

Options in Cabinetry

Cabinets aren't just for storage anymore. Available in more styles, materials, and finishes than ever before, cabinets can put the finishing touch on a room while performing the all-important function of hiding all your "stuff."

Before you start shopping for cabinets, set your priorities and research the market. Cabinet stores, showrooms, and home centers will have displays featuring various materials, finishes, and detailing. Regarding materials, cabinets can be built from solid woods, such as oak, cherry, pine, walnut, and maple, or constructed from wood composites. Solid wood is extremely durable, but composites, which are faced with a wood veneer, laminate, or metal, are generally more affordable.

Manufacturers offer cabinet lines in stock, semi-custom, and custom models. What are the differences? Read on to find out.

- **STOCK:** These are ready-to-ship styles that manufacturers keep in stock. Your kitchen designer can combine a variety of preconstructed units to fit almost any space. Stock cabinets are a smart choice if you're on a budget,

ABOVE LEFT: These kitchen cabinets are crafted of fine Honduran mahogany. The fine cabinetry makes the kitchen as beautiful as any room in the house, an important consideration because the kitchen is on view from both the living and dining rooms.

ABOVE RIGHT: Made of tumbled marble, tiles in the rectangular inset are laid horizontally while the rest are set on a diagonal. The subtle change in direction adds visual interest to the backsplash.

but you'll have fewer choices than you would with semi-custom or custom products. However, manufacturers have introduced many more storage, finish, and hardware options in recent years. On the positive side, delivery times should be speedy. Typically, stock cabinets are manufactured in 3-inch increments in standard widths of 24, 27, and 30 inches.

- **SEMI-CUSTOM:** Like stock, semi-custom cabinets are manufactured in 3-inch increments; however, they are built to order with more finishes, materials, and doors styles to choose from—so you can personalize the look at a lower cost and usually with a shorter lead time than a custom job.

- **CUSTOM:** These are built exactly to your specifications. You or your designer selects the style, size, and storage components. There are many more finishes and variations available with custom cabinets, but custom units cost significantly more than stock or semi-custom cabinetry.

Maple cabinets that feature simple detailing and hardware—along with plenty of windows—create a light, airy kitchen that welcomes all.

LEFT: The kitchen cabinetry in this prefabricated home was custom designed to reflect the homeowners' taste and storage requirements. A variety of lighting enhances the space, and skylights allow natural light to enter.

OPPOSITE: Shelves used for display and cabinet doors with multiple window panes give a kitchen character. This homeowner collected magazine clippings to find the features and materials she loved.

BELOW: Here, cabinets extend almost to the ceiling. This provides plenty of storage. To give a unified look, the refrigerator has panels that match the surrounding cabinets.

Your biggest decision in terms of cabinetry is its overall style. If your house has a traditional flavor, and you want to maintain that atmosphere in the kitchen, look for styles that have plenty of detail. You'll probably select face-framed cabinets. With face-framed cabinets, the door attaches to a support around the front of the cabinet, creating the appearance of a frame around the door. Look for cabinetry that includes furniture-like details like animal feet, corbels, or molding, for example. Units that have glass doors and open shelving give old-fashioned charm as well.

If you prefer a more modern look, frameless units may be your answer. This type of cabinet does not have a face frame; instead, a doweled construction allows the doors to fit flush with the outer edge of the cabinet box. To further enhance a smooth, contemporary look, select streamlined pulls and knobs (or no hardware at all).

KITCHENS

ABOVE: In this country-style kitchen, the cherry-stained woodwork surrounding the range was custom-built to resemble a Colonial fireplace. The narrow paneled doors on both sides of the stone conceal rollout spice racks.

TOP RIGHT: Simple cabinets come alive with the addition of an open corner unit. Glassware is prominently displayed and is easily accessible when entertaining.

BOTTOM RIGHT: The base and wall cabinets were custom-made and provide ample storage for collections of antique china. The tile insets on the backsplash date from the 1890s.

OPPOSITE: Custom cabinets, made of both maple and cherry, have a Shaker look about them. These warm tones are complemented by ash floors and soapstone counters.

LEFT: A mahogany island looks like a fine piece of furniture. It also provides a nice counterpoint to the creamy cabinets on the perimeter of the kitchen.

OPPOSITE: Moldings, columns, and corbels take this kitchen from fine to fabulous. Storage units flank the range, yet the hood is hidden behind a continuation of the cabinets.

While you're browsing the showrooms, you'll see that there's a tremendous range of finishes to choose from, and every cabinet manufacturer will offer a different selection. From antique distressed finishes to dark stains, the finish you select also affects the style. Try to get samples of all the elements that you plan to use in your kitchen to see how they'll look together.

Once you've determined the style you like, there are more decisions to be made. Do you want a plate rack to have your dishes at the ready? Would you like pullout drawers for your pots and pans? Some manufacturers have even devised a handy low-profile shelf for lids. Other great innovations in cabinetry include lazy Susan shelves, pullout cutting boards, knife drawers, and built-in spice racks.

Whatever style and features you choose, you'll want to install cabinets of top quality. Therefore, it's important to inspect the units before they are hung. Make sure the doors and drawers are solidly constructed and open easily. Check the thickness of the shelves and sides of the cabinet boxes—¾ inch is standard—and make sure the box is square in construction. Look for concealed hinges that don't bend. Seams and joint connections should be tight. Make sure the material is consistent; however, allow for less uniformity in wood species such as hickory or cherry, where the grain is more variable.

TOP LEFT: A cinch to clean and easy on your feet and back, sheet vinyl is easy to love.

BOTTOM LEFT: A checkerboard pattern is a classic approach for the kitchen floor. It can be painted on wood floors or, as seen here, created from linoleum squares. Traditionally done in black and white, this one takes a fresh approach with yellow and blue.

ABOVE: Long lasting, practical, and stylish, wood flooring will add beauty and character to any room.

OPPOSITE: Slate tiles and wood floors intermingle in the octagonal kitchen. Two islands allow plenty of room for food preparation when two chefs share the space.

Trends in Appliances

No pun intended—today's appliances are hotter than ever. In terms of materials, stainless steel is certainly continuing in popularity. In fact, manufacturers are improving on the favorite with new products—in stainless or stainless lookalikes—that are magnetic and don't show fingerprints. Originally only found in commercial kitchens, stainless steel is now appearing in both luxury and budget homes. Glass is also appearing in appliances. Range hoods made of glass offer a sleek, modern look, while refrigerators with glass doors can work in almost any décor.

What else is new? High-tech coffeemakers and espresso machines are cropping up in today's kitchen; the newest are built right into the cabinetry to create a streamlined effect. Combining speed cooking with traditional cooking is a big trend as well. Ovens often feature convection and microwave capabilities. And warming drawers allow cooks to keep dishes hot while guests are arriving. On the other side of the spectrum, there are a few ovens on the market today that keep things cool. You could store a large turkey in the oven and keep it refrigerated until you're ready to cook it. The technology is available to actually activate your oven remotely, say, from your computer at work or from your cell phone.

Other high-tech appliances include refrigerators that have small TVs built into the door, or ones that feature monitors with Internet access. With this capability, you will be able to find a recipe online, get a grocery list for the ingredients, and e-mail the list to the supermarket.

OPPOSITE, TOP LEFT: A built-in vacuum pan in the kitchen whisks crumbs away with no stooping. A basement receptacle needs periodic emptying.

OPPOSITE CENTER : A refrigerator drawer provides additional storage for cold drinks or snacks. Fine Honduran mahogany covers the unit so that it matches the rest of the cabinets.

Safety First

While you're planning your brand-new kitchen, take advantage of the advances in technology that are making this area a safer place for your family to work and relax. Talk to your architect or builder about incorporating such features, from basics like smoke alarms and ground fault circuit interrupters to antibacterial materials and water purifiers. Even the layout and materials can help prevent accidents: Include landing areas for hot pans next to the cooktop and the oven, and consider nonslip floors, those with a textured surface.

What's more, designers and manufacturers are making it much simpler to childproof your kitchen. Here are some tips that should keep your children out of harm's way.

- Install anti-scald valves on faucets.

- Buy a range or cooktop and oven with lockout features on controls and doors.

- Round the edges of countertops and tables.

- Build in enough storage to keep small appliances out of reach, and never let cords dangle over the countertop.

- Put locks or kidproof latches on cabinets. You'll want to keep your children (especially the little ones) away from all cleaning supplies, liquor, garbage, knives, or breakables.

BOTTOM LEFT: Even if you're not a coffee drinker, you have to love this built-in unit. What a sleek and convenient way to prepare your morning elixir!

ABOVE: Microwave technology is nothing new, but today's ovens are so very chic. Here, a gentle curved door graces the stainless steel unit, which is set into a wall of cabinet storage.

KITCHENS

CHAPTER SIX

Dining Rooms

A Return to Elegance

Although many homes today have great rooms which promote casual living, some homeowners still want a formal dining space. Like fashion, trends in home design are cyclical. With that, we may see fewer open plans in the future. However, what we're seeing right now is a compromise situation: great rooms with a separate formal dining room or great rooms that include a dining area that is less casual than the rest of the living area.

Many designers attribute this trend to the fact that people are entertaining at home more than in recent years. Add to this the glamorous new hobby of cooking, where top chefs, such as Emeril, Bobby Flay, and Jamie Oliver, teach food enthusiasts their tricks of the trade on their television shows. As a result, homeowners are demanding kitchens and dining spaces that function well—and that look like a showplace when they entertain.

Perfect for candelit dinners or meals on the run, this round table is tucked into an intimate corner. The wood table with a heavy base, upholstered chairs, and bench all contribute to the rich atmosphere.

And whether the dining area is enclosed or open, we're seeing the space graced with rich materials and fine furnishings. Features like wood floors with inlaid border designs, unique faux finishes on the walls, and crystal chandeliers are what take a dining space from fine to fabulous.

The return to elegance is not limited to the rich and famous. Manufacturers are creating products for people with all different budgets. If you flip through a Pottery Barn catalog, for example, you'll see reasonably priced chandeliers, velvet curtains, and beautiful dining pieces. Also, because you can find affordable products, you don't have to worry as much when red wine spills or someone bangs into the table by accident. This allows the formal dining space to have a casual, welcoming feeling, even though it has a luxurious look.

BELOW: Although this dining room has a modern flavor, the oversized table and mixture of Chinese slat-back and tufted chairs create a gracious space that welcomes guests.

OPPOSITE: A pared-down dining room exudes elegance by including only special pieces and décor. Walls feature grasscloth of pale silk with a delicate Asian-inspired painting of cherry blossoms (visible in the lower right corner).

DINING ROOMS

Creating the Proper Environment

When planning your dining room, work out the practical details prior to purchasing that antique tea set. Ask yourself: How will this space be used? How many people does the room need to hold? Is there room for guests to spill out into the living area? Think about the proximity to the kitchen. You'll need to be able to bring food in and out of the dining area easily. Consider the traffic flow when you'll be serving food and your guests will be gathering around the table. If you already have a table and chairs, make sure the room will not only allow for the furnishings, but also have enough room for a person to pass by when a chair is pulled out from the table.

RIGHT: Set in a ski house in Vermont, this dining room exhibits the perfect balance of casual living with a touch of elegance. A large wood dining table and leather-wrapped chairs welcome dinner guests.

BELOW: This dining room's traditional elements include a white oak floor with an inset border, coffered ceiling, wainscoting, crown molding, and a built-in china cabinet. The chairs are upholstered in silk slipcovers.

Originally from New Orleans, this couple gave their Massachusetts dining room a French flavor. Yellow walls warm up the room, while an eighteenth-century French chandelier holds thick wax candles with electrical fittings to illuminate the setting.

If you want to make this room special, think about focal points. Perhaps you want to include a fireplace in close proximity to your dining space. Also, what will the windows look like? You might want to create a bay window or an oversized window as a focal point in the room. Next, think about how you'll dress the window. Do you want to leave the windows bare and let the architecture speak for itself, or do you prefer shades or draperies—or maybe just a simple valence to give a finished look? Here's a good trick: If you have a room with ceilings of standard height, you can give the dining room a sense of height and grandeur by running your curtain rod as close to the ceiling as possible rather than at the top of the window. This will heighten the room visually. Flowing draperies that pool a bit at the bottom always add elegance to a room. Here, too, you needn't spend a fortune. You can buy inexpensive fabric (measure the height of the room and add about 12 inches) and just hem the edges and attach curtain loops to the top. Also, decide whether you need to draw the curtains. If they are just for decorative purposes, you don't need that much fabric to create panels to frame the views.

Furnishing Your Space

Clearly, the dining room table and the surrounding chairs will occupy most of the space in your dining area, and therefore, these pieces will set the tone of the room. Decide, then, between a formal and an informal space. If you love a real casual atmosphere, seek out a special flea market find, perhaps a table made from old pine floors from a barn. If you lean toward a more formal feeling, look for a classic mahogany table with plenty of detail. Or for a modern room, consider materials other than wood, such as glass, metal—or even concrete.

Think about the shape of your table, as well as how the shape will change with the leaves. Do you like the straightforward form of a rectangle, or do you prefer a round table? An oval table is always a nice choice, because it takes up the same amount of space as a rectangle, but gives a softer look. One way to determine what you like is to take the floor plan and draw in the different shapes. See what shape suits the space. Consider, too, how the chairs will fit around the table. Keep in mind you should have about 2 feet behind each chair to allow guests to comfortably walk around the chairs.

Most retailers will have tables on display, so you can see how many chairs can be set around the table. However, if you can't see the table in person, the rule of thumb is that you need at least 24 inches per place setting—and 30 inches is even better. If you're limited on space, a 40-inch round should accommodate four people. Conversely, if you have a large space, you may want to consider an 11 x 4-foot table to seat twelve.

Once you've selected the style you want and the size, it's important to check the quality of the pieces you buy. If you're buying a dining room set—this might include the table,

The paneled archway leading into the dining room complements the traditional crown molding and the five-foot-high wainscoting. The ceiling is nine feet high, giving the room a spacious feeling.

OPPOSITE: Formal dining rooms don't have to be stuffy. This dining room is casual in decor, but the fact that it's a separate room gives the space a sense of elegance and formality.

BELOW: To add warmth to a log home in Telluride, Colorado, the interior designer dressed the walls in the dining room in chocolate-brown leather.

chairs, and a sideboard—make sure that the pieces are sturdy and are well constructed. Ask if the pieces are solid wood or plywood with a veneer. Take note most pieces of furniture—even the finest ones—have veneers. A veneer is a thin layer that covers the surface of the piece. The difference between high and low quality furniture is the material beneath the veneer. Another word of caution: Read the labels carefully. For instance, a wood piece may be described as having a "mahogany finish." This does not mean that the table is made from solid mahogany. It may in fact be made from pine, which is a much softer, less expensive wood, and then finished with a dark stain.

For sideboards, see how the piece is constructed. Look at the joints. The best joints are dovetail, where the joint looks like teeth and is meshed together, and mortise and tenon, where one piece fits into the pocket of another. Next, check the drawers. Do they slide out and in easily? Do they have a track? What is the track made of—wood or metal? In general, metal tracks allow the drawers to slide smoothly. Look inside the drawers—are they lined? Some sideboards include velvet-lined drawers or have separators to hold serving pieces.

Regarding the chairs, you'll obviously want something that complements the style of the table. However, there are certainly no rules. Some of the most charming dining rooms have a collection of chairs that range from handcrafted wood chairs found in foreign lands to store-bought upholstered pieces. Look for chairs you just love. Make sure you sit in them to see if they're comfortable. Also, check that the height of the chair will work well with your table.

ABOVE: In the casual eating area in the kitchen, Early American antiques lend warm, country charm. A large armoire provides extra storage space.

LEFT: The back of the kitchen fireplace forms one wall of the dining room. The ceiling is made of pine, which will become richer and darker with age. The dining room's walls were covered in sheetrock and painted in order to keep the abundance of wood throughout the house from becoming overwhelming.

OPPOSITE: For the dining room, Mission-style chairs and a simple table complement the Craftsman design of this Boulder, Colorado home. The architectural details in the space are original.

OPPOSITE: A durable wood table and wood chairs sit atop the dining room carpet of stain-resistant nylon. The furnishings are perfect for the mountainside ski house, where friends and family want a no-fuss atmosphere.

BELOW: The dining room has a contemporary feeling to accommodate the artwork and the sleek handcrafted bronze bases of the ten-foot-long glass table. The floor has been raised so the ceilings are low, eight-feet high as opposed to ten-feet high elsewhere in the home. The step-up room gives the area a separate, intimate feeling.

Quick Changes

Your dining room can be dressed up or dressed down. Here are some easy changes:

- ADD SLIPCOVERS. If, for example, you have rustic wood chairs and want a more polished look, don't purchase new chairs, simply dress up the old chairs with slipcovers. Slipcovers are also an easy way to add color to a room.

- DON A TABLECLOTH. Buy a number of inexpensive tablecloths and change your table from season to season or for different holidays or parties. Consider red for Valentine's Day and green or yellow for the first day of spring.

- ROTATE YOUR ARTWORK. This is a great trick to update a room quickly. Your artwork need not be expensive. Frame some black-and-white photos for a modern look or press leaves and flowers to create botanical prints for a more traditional feeling.

- CREATE DIFFERENT CENTERPIECES. For the fall, fill a wood bowl with mini-pumpkins, and in the summer, go to your farmers' market and get some huge sunflowers to place in a galvanized bucket. If you're lucky enough to live near the beach or simply love that seaside feeling, make an arrangement using hurricane vases of different sizes and filling them with sand and seashells. Hurricane vases as well as clear glass vases are excellent decorative accessories. For a sophisticated holiday look use cranberries as a base for red amaryllis in a clear glass cylinder. Finish it off with a gold wire ribbon.

- CHANGE THE LIGHTING. Think about adding a table lamp to the corner of your dining room. This will create a small focal point and set the area aglow. Or why not give your chandelier a fresh look by changing or adding different lampshades? There are so many to choose from—you can even find shades with small stones dangling from the rims.

ABOVE: Columns and arches carry this home's Mediterranean exterior style into the interior. Seen through an archway from the foyer, the dining room is warmed by mocha-colored walls and gold silk draperies. The flooring is Portuguese limestone.

TOP RIGHT: What began as a standard remodel evolved into the transformation of a brick Colonial ranch house into a French country farmhouse. The hutch is a French piece that was handed down from a family member; the sunflowers complete the country ambiance.

BOTTOM RIGHT: This dining room, enlarged during a remodel by borrowing space from an adjoining hall, features an antique table long enough to seat more than a dozen people. The door, moved from another part of the house during the remodel, still bears traces of its original paint, providing a link to the original 200-year-old home.

OPPOSITE: An elegant chandelier includes lampshades with subtle details. The dining area also features hammered copper above the mantel to really make the room sparkle.

DINING ROOMS

Lighting Your Way

The lighting in your dining room is a crucial element in your scheme. These days, some of the most interesting rooms feature disparate styles. For example, in a shabby chic scheme you might see a pitted wood table below a sparkling crystal chandelier. You may need a combination of lighting in the room, like recessed light to illuminate the space and sconces to offer ambience.

Second only to chandeliers, pendant lights are very popular today. These work well in more casual or modern dining spaces. You can hang a large pendant centered in the space or, say, three small ones running down the center of the ceiling.

Chandeliers are certainly the most traditional choice for dining spaces. Luckily, there is a range of choices on the market. Wrought-iron candlestick types offer an uncluttered look, while crystal fixtures adorned with multifaceted prisms create an elegant atmosphere. If you purchase an antique fixture, inspect it carefully and inquire about its history. Make sure that there are no missing pieces, especially when the fixture has numerous glass prisms, and be

ABOVE: Is it inspired by Asian designs, or Frank Lloyd Wright? The hanging light fixture certainly makes a statement in the otherwise neutral dining room.

OPPOSITE: Featuring such elegant details as paneled walls and an Oriental rug, the dining room also includes a touch of whimsy: The lampshades have a leopard pattern.

OPPOSITE: When you think of a formal dining room, certainly a crystal chandelier comes to mind. Here is a true beauty that makes the dramatic red room shine.

RIGHT: The candle-style chandelier is electrified. Its unique shape—possibly made from old pieces of metal—makes it a distinctive piece.

BELOW: Above the simply designed table and chairs hangs an ornate metal chandelier. Its scroll design is repeated in the candleholder on the fireplace wall.

sure the wiring is up-to-date. Old wiring is unsafe and may cause a fire.

Whatever style you select, place the lights on dimmers. Dimmers allow you to create the atmosphere you like. Today, there are even automated systems that allow you to set the lighting from a remote location. These high-tech lighting systems can also raise and lower the shades, choose which lights are on, and select the level of lighting that each gives. When it comes to lighting, don't forget about the switchplates. Today's manufacturers offer a range of colors and styles, but you must decide if you want your switchplates to be camouflaged into the wall or be a decorative feature.

CHAPTER SEVEN

Master Suites

Creating a Private Retreat

Many days, the press of responsibilities manages to infringe upon practically every corner of our lives. We answer phone calls in the car, eat meals between children's sporting events, and play constant catch-up with deadlines at work. Take heart. Amidst all this hubbub, there is a refuge: the master suite. For many, this private haven provides just about the only peace and quiet of the day.

It's hard to believe that prior to the 1960s, the idea of the master suite had not yet emerged. Homes had modest bedrooms and purely functional baths. Today, we yearn for bedrooms that are luxurious sanctuaries and baths that feature all the latest amenities.

One of four bedroom suites, the luxurious master suite includes architectural details such as a tray ceiling and crown molding.

LEFT: A gilded bench set in front of the bed lends a regal touch. The sumptuous suite also features glazed walls, bed coverings of silk and matelasse, and floor-to-ceiling curtains.

OPPOSITE: Even the corners of this master suite offer luxury. Here, an overstuffed chaise and a floor lamp provide the perfect place to relax and read a book.

BELOW: No master suite is complete without a grand master bath. Here, mosaic tiles surround the tub and damask and silk curtains frame the views.

Locating the Suite

When building a new home or remodeling an existing one, think about where your master suite should be located. Do you have young children? If so, you will want the suite to be near them, so you can attend to their needs in the middle of the night. On the other hand, if you have teenagers, you may want your suite as far away from them as possible. Consider, too, your age and health. Nowadays, many homes have the master suite on the first floor. This gives accessibility to people who don't feel comfortable climbing stairs—or those who physically cannot.

Dividing Up the Suite

Your ideal master suite should be both beautiful and efficient. Therefore, it's important to divide the space properly. For the bedroom, you'll need the following:

- **SLEEPING AREA:** Obviously, this space will include the bed. Choose the size bed you like and determine where it will fit best in the plan. Here are some typical measurements.

     As you can see, you have a lot of choices for your master suite bed. California Queen and King beds work well for tall people. Keep in mind, however, it's easier to find linens for the standard twin, full, queen, and king sizes.

MATTRESS TYPE	WIDTH	LENGTH
Twin	39 inches	75 inches
Extra-long twin	39 inches	80 inches
Full/Double	54 inches	75 inches
Queen	60 inches	80 inches
Olympic Queen	66 inches	80 inches
California Queen	60 inches	84 inches
King	76 inches	80 inches
California King	72 inches	84 inches

At the top of most homeowners' wish lists is a private, soothing master suite. This one looks out over the backyard and has double doors leading to a patio sheltered by the house's main roofline.

MASTER SUITES

LEFT: Located off the kitchen and the great room, the master bedroom feels as though it's part of a giant apartment. A midnight snack is always only a few steps away.

BELOW: The master bath features an open shower area and a corner tub. Both areas include steps. It's important that when designing with steps in the bath, you use only slip-resistant flooring.

Travertine tile forms a handsome surround for the master bedroom fireplace. The colors from the hearth are repeated throughout the house.

Don't forget that you'll probably need bedside tables. At a minimum, these require an additional 12 inches of space on either side of your bed. And make sure that you're not blocking closet doors that swing open or an entryway.

- **DRESSING AREA:** If you have the luxury of space, you can reserve a place just for getting dressed. Perhaps you have an area near your closet that would work well or even an unused corner that could become your dressing space. This area should include a full-length mirror and be near your closet.

- **STORAGE:** The ultimate luxury is an oversized walk-in closet (or two of them), outfitted with all kinds of storage gear—shelving, rods, drawers, shoe holders, and the like. Some walk-in closets in new houses are the same size as bedrooms in urban apartments. Check your floor plan to see if a walk-in closet is included. Note how the doors open. Do they swing out into the room? Are they pocket doors? Or accordions? This design will affect how you can outfit the rest of the space. For example, you might be better off having a pocket door if you have a lot of furniture that you'd like to include in the bedroom. However, a pocket door will require that you have the appropriate square footage on at least one side of the door, so the door can slide into the wall. Doors that swing out into the room take up more space, but they do offer a handsome look and are sturdier than accordion doors. Talk to your architect about having the door swing into the closet, rather than out into the room.

The ceiling in this master suite has a barrel vaulted inset for added interest, and the adjoining master bath has a barrel vaulted ceiling. A balcony with a view of the Colorado mountains expands the bedroom's size.

RIGHT: The columns next to the bed serve as clever torchères with side reading lights and general lighting shining from above. The walls are covered with canvas in a glistening taupe; the slight shimmer is repeated in the upholstery of the custom-designed headboard. The space feels serene, a result of the clever mix of neutral-toned textures and fabrics.

BELOW: The tub in this master bath is surrounded by a steam shower on the right and a fireplace on the left. A pocket door closes off the entrance. The tub is situated to take advantage of one of the many spectacular views from the house.

In addition to closets, you'll need a location for a dresser or two. When you're deciding on space for your dresser, you should also determine whether you need a surface to put things on. Will you have a television in your master suite? Where will it be placed? If you plan to get a plasma TV, perhaps you don't need a horizontal surface; you'll just need the wall space.

- **SITTING AREA:** What could be more delightful than having a plush armchair and ottoman or a chaise longue set in the corner of your master suite? If your floor plan allows, create a sitting area with your favorite chair and a light for curling up with a good book, watching TV, sitting by a fireplace, or just taking a midday nap.

ABOVE: To enjoy this fabulous view through the stunning round window, the designer selected classic seating and a casual woven coffee table to decorate the sitting area in the master bedroom.

LEFT: The furnishings in this master bedroom blend Tuscan with California style: rich, dark woods and breezy off-whites.

- **WORK ZONE:** Depending on your habits, you might want a spot for taking care of everyday business in your master suite. A small desk or even a simple table and a chair will do the trick. It's nice to create this workspace beneath a window, so you can enjoy the view while paying bills or writing thank-you notes.

- **BATH:** For the bath, you'll need room for a tub and shower area, a place for grooming and washing up, and the toilet and bidet spot. See the chapter on Baths (page 161) for more details.

RIGHT: There's plenty of room to sit and read in this master suite. The blue-and-yellow color scheme is carried over into the bathroom as well.

BELOW: Inspired by the water and sky just outside, pale blue upholstered chairs and an overstuffed ottoman provide a cozy seating area in the master bedroom, which has views of the Atlantic Ocean.

LEFT: Large and luxurious, this bath is flooded with light from the huge casement window and skylight. The arched windows were modeled after those the homeowners had seen on farmhouses in Europe.

BELOW: A remodel to this home allowed for a bigger master suite and bath. A new bedroom sitting area was included, and the French doors lead out to a second-story terrace. The goal with the interior décor was to create a welcoming and homey atmosphere.

An abundance of wood, ever-present in a log home, is offset here by a mixture of other materials and textures, such as leather, wrought iron, and glass. This is one of two master suites in the home; both have private balconies overlooking the mountains.

MASTER SUITES

ABOVE: If you want a tailored look, consider blinds like these. They just fade into the background of your decorating scheme.

LEFT: Silhouette shades have a translucent effect. This gives you privacy while allowing light to enter the space.

Get a Luxury Look

Creating a luxurious master suite doesn't have to cost a fortune. Below are a few ways to stay within your budget while getting the suite of your dreams.

- **GOING UNDER COVER:** The most personal space in your home should be the coziest of retreats, and since most of your time in this room is probably spent in bed, it makes sense to pay careful attention to your bedding, both in terms of comfort and style. And you'll find that styles abound: beautifully embroidered shams, exquisite quilts and coverlets, and impossibly soft imported sheets, all easy to coordinate. Check the labels on your bedding; there are several things to consider.

  Start by looking at the fabric content. Is it a percale, the most common type of cotton sheet; a jersey, or knitted cotton; a sateen; flannel; or a blend of cotton and synthetics? Next, check the thread count. Thread count is defined as the number of yarns in the weft added to the number of yarns in the warp in an area that is one square inch. What does this all mean to you? The higher the thread count, the softer your sheets. Percales have the lowest thread counts, starting at 180, while luxury percales range from about 220 threads per square inch to 270. From that point, sateen, which has a satiny hand, takes over—with thread counts reaching as high as 440 or more in the finest European textiles. Egyptian cotton has a reputation for high quality since it offers durability, luster, and softness, which is the result of long, staple fibers. But check to make sure that a product labeled Egyptian cotton is 100 percent Egyptian cotton, since sometimes that labeling applies to sheets with a much smaller percentage of the high-quality cotton. In the United States, Pima cotton is considered the highest quality. If a sheet is

A velvet pillow mingles with a chenille throw and pillows to create an elegant look. An upholstered headboard adds a splash of color and complements the wall tones.

ABOVE: Embroidered pillowcases and sheets provide a nice amount of detail without appearing overwhelming. You can even create something similar by sewing on interesting trim to white cases.

LEFT: A cashmere throw adds a touch of luxury to any bedroom. Here, a pink one with fringe dresses up the all-white bed.

labeled Supima cotton, it is guaranteed to be 100 percent Pima cotton.

In terms of style, bed linens don't have to match. You can shop sales for sheets, dust ruffles, shams, and blankets that pick up one tone in the main pattern of the comforter, for example. Then, tie it all together with a lightweight throw placed at the end of the bed.

For a luxurious look, pile your bed with masses of pillows or show off a combination of heirloom linens. Prefer a more low-key effect? Choose pillowcases and sheets that have embroidered trim in a color that matches the walls or a blanket. Or mimic the look for less: Sew strips of cotton braid or fabric in contrasting shades on plain sheets. Remember, whether tailored or traditional, it's whatever makes you comfortable.

Large windows let in plenty of sunlight in this master bedroom. The venetian blinds virtually disappear when opened, leaving only the sheer curtains to filter light. Topped by a billowing canopy, the bed is opposite a fireplace with a cozy seating area.

- **WINDOWS THAT WOW:** When it comes to window treatments, the possibilities are endless, even in the fast-and-easy category. If you're looking for soft elegance across a wall of windows, balloon shades may be the perfect solution; you'll find many ready-made or made-to-order in catalogs. For a more tailored look, consider buying miniblinds, shutters, or Roman shades that complement your room. Cellular shades are another option. These admit light while blocking unwanted views—or viewers.

  If you have many large windows in your bedroom and bath (and not such a large budget), while you're shopping for your sheets, pick up a few to transform into draperies. Satin, eyelet, striped, checked, or floral print sheets look as nice on a window as they do on a bed.

And you don't have to be a seamstress to make this option work. Just invest in a decorative curtain rod, cut open the ends of the deep hem at the top of the sheet and pull the rod through. Or simply drape the sheet over the rod to create a soft swag. And to dress up what you have, add new contrasting tiebacks—you can even use ribbons or scarves.

- **MAGIC CARPET:** Few elements make as dramatic an impact on a bedroom as well-chosen carpets and rugs. Wall-to-wall is a comfortable, beautiful choice, but it must be professionally installed. If you prefer something that you can do yourself, consider carpet squares. These have adhesive backs and can be laid down in different patterns. Or purchase a rug that's almost as big as your room to give the effect of wall-to-wall carpeting. In an instant the whole space will seem softer and more inviting.

- **MATERIALS MATTER:** Plentiful use of fabrics gives a bedroom a soft, serene look, so be creative. For example, craft a headboard by upholstering a screen. Or to add romance, you can create an airy canopy by running some inexpensive netting from mounted drapery brackets on the ceiling above the bed to a pair on the wall behind it.

  For a darling night table with secret storage, top a file cabinet with a round of fiberboard, then drape the unit with a long, circular skirt. Revamp a boring dresser with a table runner in a favorite print. Limit the number of prints you use in the space, as too many will make the room feel busy rather than relaxing. Look for fabrics that are washable and mix and match different textures in the space.

- **DRAMATIC DETAILS:** Select cabinet knobs and hardware for your bedroom dresser and bath cabinets that add sparkle. Whether you go for sleek stainless steel handles, glass knobs, or something whimsical, such as drawer pulls shaped like dragonflies, hardware can lend immediate personality. Before you trek out to the stores or begin to browse online, determine the number of knobs and pulls you need. Next, take measurements to make sure your choice will work. Think about comfort—does it feel good in your hand?—as well as style. Found the perfect hardware? Take ten minutes to install these favorites, and every time you open the cabinets, you're sure to feel pleased.

OPPOSITE: Heavy draperies can be drawn when privacy is needed. During the day, they frame the spectacular view and soften the architecture.

CHAPTER EIGHT

Guest and Children's Rooms

Fresh paint and wallcoverings can turn a nondescript bedroom into a cozy haven for children. The window seat, old-fashioned stencils, and child-size wicker furniture are favorite features of this pretty girl's bedroom.

Creating a Separate Suite

In the 1800s, it was very common for the wealthy to have a guest house. Today, we don't see as many as we did in the past. The trend has shifted to creating guest quarters or guest suites within the main house. These suites can just simply be set off to one side of the house or separated by a breezeway or long hall. You can also create a separation by having your master suite on one level and the guest suite on another.

The idea of a separate suite is also one that appeals to parents with children living at home. It allows for a separation from the parents and gives the children a sense of autonomy. The suite may even include its own entrance, so older kids can come and go without disturbing the parents. Of course, if your children require a watchful eye, having a separate suite may not be the best situation for your home.

Make Guests Feel at Home

Once you've determined the location of your suite, design the space so that guests feel welcome. Your location may dictate your design choices. For example, if you live in a cold climate, try to incorporate a fireplace into your guest suite and outfit the space with cozy furnishings, such as flannel sheets and wall-to-wall carpet or a plush rug. If your house is by the beach, think about a nautical theme for your furnishings.

No matter what the design scheme, make sure to create an adequate lighting plan. You should have overall, ambient lighting—perhaps set on a dimmer to create the proper atmosphere—as well as task lighting. The task lighting should be placed above the bed, seating, or desk area to allow for reading or working.

ABOVE LEFT: An adjoining bathroom to the child's bedroom features polka-dotted wallpaper, flower-shaped pulls, and hardworking laminate cabinets.

ABOVE RIGHT: Placing the children's suite on the same floor as the master suite allows parents to keep a careful eye on their children. Striped painted walls give a crisp look to the bedroom.

OPPOSITE: This guest room features a stained-pine, tongue-and-groove ceiling, and wrought iron accents, including the curtain rods and blanket rack. The stack of suitcases is a whimsical touch, serving as storage and a small table next to the chair.

GUEST AND CHILDREN'S ROOMS

BELOW: In a corner of this log home sits a tub surrounded by cream limestone. It's positioned for bathers to enjoy the mountain vistas beyond.

ABOVE: Replacing a standard wall mirror with two decoratively designed units helps make this bath more appealing to its visitors.

Guest suites generally include a bathroom. For this space, consider hotel-like amenities, such as a whirlpool tub, a steam shower, and radiant heating. If your budget or space doesn't allow for these luxuries, small touches like a towel warmer or French-milled soaps give guests the feeling of a deluxe accommodation.

Some suites have their own kitchen. If there's not enough room for a full kitchen, one might include an under-the-counter refrigerator in the bathroom, or a refrigerator drawer in the bedroom. An area designated for making coffee allows guests to have their morning coffee prior to seeing their hosts.

This guest suite makes its visitors feel as if they're staying in the Swiss Alps. For this Colorado bedroom, a hand-painted whimsical bed is the focal point of the log room.

GUEST AND CHILDREN'S ROOMS

OPPOSITE: The guest room in this 200-year-old house was expanded to include a window seat and a clothes closet. The closet door and hardware are original, moved from elsewhere in the house during a remodel.

ABOVE: Tucked beneath an eave, a cushioned banquette is the perfect spot for a child to curl up in. Monogrammed drawers underneath the banquette provide additional storage.

Just for Kids

Whether you've designated separate suites for your children or just one room, designing for kids requires a lot of thought and planning. Your child's room should be a place where he or she can play, create, and rest comfortably and safely. The age of your child will drive the design. If your child is old enough to have some input, talk to your child about what she wants in the space. Ask what colors he likes. Flip through catalogs with your child to see what appeals to him. Sometimes a child cannot verbalize what he likes, but is able to show you her preferences. Does your child have a favorite pastime? If your son loves sports, certainly this is an easy theme to commit to. You can find all kinds of sport-theme fabrics, bedding, and wallpaper. But if you prefer a room that's more sophisticated, keep the space neutral—and then add accessories that give character. For example, rather than a dresser painted with little boys playing baseball, purchase a plain dresser and then just change the knobs— to baseballs and bats—to add some fun.

This sitting area is intended for the teenage children of the homeowners. Brimming with a deluxe entertainment system, the room is situated at the opposite end of a hall from the master suite, providing a buffer from any noisy gatherings. Built-in bunks accommodate guests for sleepovers.

New cribs must meet the Consumer Product Safety Commission standards. If you have an antique, make sure that the slats are no more than 2⅜ inches apart, that there aren't any loose parts, and that the crib is not covered with lead paint.

Once you've figured out what the scheme will be, let your child be involved. In general, school age children about three to eleven years of age begin to develop their own preferences. Involving your child in the process by picking colors, choosing sheets, or even helping with a stenciled border encourages him to be imaginative and creative. In turn, the child will also feel more comfortable in his room and will have gained a new sense of pride and accomplishment.

However, before you start purchasing cans of paint and buying bedding, consider these factors below.

- BE SAFE. If you have a toddler running around, there are all sorts of precautions you must take. Make sure that bookcases and furnishings cannot be pulled down on top of your child. There are gadgets you can buy to secure the furnishings to the wall. Block all electrical outlets. Watch out for cords on blinds. These should be out of reach of the child. Looped cords are especially dangerous in terms of a child choking. If possible, install plush carpet to soften those inevitable falls that toddlers have. Nightlights are also helpful for both kids and for parents checking in. If you feel it's necessary, there are experts that will "childproof" your home for a fee. Check your local yellow pages for a listing.

- **LEAVE ROOM TO GROW.** When designing a space for an infant, you may want to outfit it with things like nursery rhymes and teddy bears. However, hold that maternal (or paternal) instinct! Your child is not always going to be a toddler. Your teenager-to-be may not appreciate the all-pink room with a doll motif on the walls. With this in mind, create a shell that's somewhat neutral. For example, paint the walls and then embellish them with a wallpaper border that can be easily changed. For floors, choose a rug or carpet that is not too juvenile.

For furniture, look for pieces that can grow with the child. Some cribs, for example, can be converted into a small bed. Also, rather than a changing table per se, find a dresser that does double duty. Many dressers can have a changing pad attached to them. Then, when the child gets older, the changing table is removed.

If two children are sharing a room, there are a few different options. Twin beds dressed in coordinating sheets give a room a charming quality. Bunk beds are great if you're short on space. If the bunks don't already have a ladder, add a decorative ladder to help a child climb up to the top bunk. Another idea is a trundle

Melon-colored walls with stars in bright hues set the tone for this bedroom. Furnishings, however, are white, so that as the child grows the scheme can be easily changed without buying all new pieces.

GUEST AND CHILDREN'S ROOMS

Tucked under the eaves on the third floor, this charming spare bedroom is a perfect guest room. The radiator cover was made by a local carpenter.

bed, where one bed can be tucked beneath another when not in use. This can be a little more work for kids to roll one bed beneath the other. Trundles work better for guest quarters or for college-age kids who need to use the beds only when they're home on a break.

- **STORE MORE.** As most parents know, children accumulate an enormous amount of stuff. From stacking rings to soccer balls, all your child's toys and gadgets need to be stored or displayed. Fortunately, storage is big business, which gives you many products from which to choose. In addition to plenty of closet space, you should include pieces like bookcases, shelving, or an armoire in your child's room. To organize the space, provide lots of

bins and baskets that are color coded, so kids can easily clean up their space. For example, all cars and trucks go in the red bin, while blocks are placed in the yellow basket. A combination of high and low shelves gives parents the opportunity to keep things in reach—and more importantly—out of reach.

Once the child is a bit older, the bins can be used for storing school books and any awards or favorite trinkets can be neatly displayed on the shelves.

When your toddler becomes a teenager, he's not going to want a cutout duck for his headboard. Here, classically designed wood beds can be used at any age.

● **CREATE A PLAY SPACE.** Although you may create a room that you absolutely love, keep in mind your child will be actually using this space. Look for materials that are durable and low maintenance. You might adore a fine needlepoint carpet in a pale shade, but think about how you'll feel when your baby spits up on it, or your teenager comes home with muddy shoes.

Make sure there is adequate floor space in the room for kids just to play, pretend, devise puppet shows, etc. There should be room for your baby boy to push his toy train back and forth, and for your little girl to have an easel for her artwork—or vice versa.

- **DEVISE A WORK ZONE.** In addition to a play area, include a spot for an older child to do homework, like a desk or a simple table. Don't forget about lighting. It's important to incorporate task lighting in areas where your children read or do their homework.

This teenager's room is designed with plenty of storage and open space. The blue-and-white color scheme imbues the room with an airy, youthful ambiance. The white shutters contribute to the crispness of the decor.

RIGHT: Soft furnishings and a rug will provide some comfort when your child is attempting to walk. Also, nail bookcases and armoires to the wall if they could tip over on the child.

BELOW: Easily stackable, these colorful boxes make ideal containers for everything from stuffed animals to rubber balls.

BOTTOM: Children need spaces to play. Here, kid-size chairs give a place for bunny and bear to enjoy a spot of tea. Vinyl floors offer a bit of cushion in case a toddler takes a tumble.

- **KEEP IT CLEAN.** Even with all the toys, cars, books, and teddy bears, you'll want this room to look somewhat organized and neat. As we mentioned above, make sure you've planned enough storage space to keep clutter at bay. And to avoid marring walls, choose paints and wallcoverings specifically made for children. Paints that have a glossy finish allow parents to wipe walls clean when sticky hands muck up the space. When picking fabrics, choose those that have texture or pattern, because they are less likely to show dirt.

Kids' baths

Don't leave your creative juices in the bedroom; the bath is also a place to have a bit of fun. Mickey Mouse tiles might not help the resale value of your house, but a brightly colored bath often is a conversation piece. Primary colors will work well if you have a girl or boy— and it's also suitable if this bathroom becomes a guest bath in the future. If you're not keen on brights, consider glass tiles on the walls. These come in muted shades and give a bath a sophisticated look.

Incorporate storage in the bath for towels and favorite shampoos. Vanities with low maintenance counters are a great choice for kids. In small bathrooms, consider a pedestal sink, and try to incorporate a medicine cabinet or shelves to stow the kids' bath stuff.

Have fun in the space. Rubber ducks on display, for instance, can add a touch of whimsy to a child's bath, but can be removed when they grow up, or when you'd like to turn the bath into one for adults. If you're not sure you want a bright color on the walls, consider just painting one wall or the ceiling in a spirited hue. Shower curtains come in all kinds of designs. It's nice to let your child pick out his or her favorite. However, if you don't want the Little Mermaid greeting you, limit your child's choices. Perhaps a bold print or a curtain adorned with ribbons or pom-poms will be more to your liking. A playful bath mat—maybe in a cheerful shape like a fish—will make your kids smile, especially when they are trying to avoid brushing their teeth or washing up.

Lastly, create a bath that's safe. Watch out for slippery wet floors. Rubber bath mats placed in the tub or shower as well as nonslip floors will hopefully prevent accidents. And make sure that the bath is properly lit and that all electrical outlets are up to code. If you're remodeling, replace old electrical outlets with ones that shut off automatically if they are exposed to water. With toddlers, block any outlets completely and childproof the toilet. Curious little ones will explore even the most unusual places.

ABOVE: For a little girl's bath, butterflies are stenciled on the wall to add whimsy. This is a great do-it-yourself project. Just make sure that your artwork is in an area that's not overly moist.

OPPOSITE: Requiring almost no maintenance, the easy-care vinyl floor in this teens' bathroom stands up gracefully to spills and damp towels left on the floor.

CHAPTER NINE

Baths

The abundance of wood in the bathroom is offset by a mixture of other materials and textures, including wrought iron, granite, stainless steel, and large windows.

Space Planning

Before you pick out dual pedestal sinks or towel racks, think about how you'll lay out the space. Allot enough room for your daily activities, and then approximate the space for each zoned area.

- **TUB AND SHOWER AREA:** When you look at your floor plan, see if your architect has included a separate tub and shower. Many homes today have a whirlpool tub as the focal point of the bath and then a stall shower set in a corner of the space. However, the trend is shifting to making the shower the main event. Many whirlpool owners are finding that they don't really have the time to use the whirlpool tub, and shower systems are all the rage. Look for units that offer multiple heads, steam options, and massaging elements.

- **GROOMING AND SINK AREA:** The choices in sinks have never been so diverse, from the traditional pedestals to washbasins to trough sinks that span the length of the counter. Here, you'll need to think about form and function. Do you want two sinks to ease the morning rush? Do you need a long counter for your cosmetics? If so, pedestal sinks are not for you. Not least of all come the decisions for the lighting and fixtures for the space.

- **TOILET AND BIDET AREA:** Privacy is certainly the main issue for this area. Do you want a separate stall for the toilet? Perhaps a half wall will provide the separation you need. A clever way to close off a toilet area is with a door that runs on a track. Aligning the toilet and shower areas will allow doors closing off each to run on the same track which will give a streamlined look while setting the functional areas apart from the rest of the space.

Focus on Design

Attention to detail in your bath will certainly pay off. There are so many ways to take a bath from ordinary to extraordinary. Start by selecting a color palette. To create a Zen-like atmosphere, select pale hues. However, the bath needn't be all the same color. Mixing colors and tone adds visual interest to a neutral scheme.

Next, study your floor plan. How many windows are in the bath? Think about both privacy and how much artificial light you will need. To let in natural light, but keep out unwanted viewers, consider translucent shades.

ABOVE: Divided-light windows frame the view out the master bathroom window. The floor tiles and tiled wainscoting adds a handsome, polished look to the bath.

RIGHT: Because the bath includes neutral tones—bluish-gray walls, white cabinets, and a light wood ceiling—the antique table used in the center of the room becomes the focal point.

OPPOSITE: French doors topped by a matching transom open onto a bath with a thirteen-foot ceiling. The window in the peaked gable brings in more natural light, and wall sconces offer a decorative touch. The floor has radiant floor heating.

You'll require overall light as well as task lighting for putting on makeup or styling your hair. Talk to your architect about developing a lighting scheme that will work well in your bath. Also, you'll want to illuminate the space in a warm, inviting way—steer clear of fluorescent bulbs that make you look pale and pasty and flood the room with harsh light.

Think about materials for walls and floors. Here are a few:

- TILE AND STONE: Today's tile and stone floors concentrate on texture and offer options for designing a floor that reflects one's own style. Many manufacturers offer coordinating wall and floor tile collections that emphasize accent tiles and create interesting focal points on the floor. The trend toward larger tiles that range anywhere from 16 to 24 inches is evident in both compact and expansive baths. If one selects the color thoughtfully, it is possible to graciously incorporate a tile as large as 18 inches into a small powder room. As an alternative to a floor fashioned exclusively in stone, ceramic and stone tiles are combined to produce a chic look at an affordable price. Porcelain ceramic tiles now are made to resemble natural marble and travertine. The most fashionable tile color palettes highlight the earthy tones prevalent in nature: variations of updated neutrals, warm greens, golds, and browns.

- **LAMINATE:** Laminate floors continue to mimic natural materials. It's a practical surface with endless design possibilities. Make sure that your laminate floor is appropriate for the bath. Some laminates do not resist water as well as others.

- **WOOD:** Wood always offers natural beauty, but proper sealing is the key to this look for the bath. Certain woods may also require continued maintenance. However, if the wood is properly treated, it can even be used as a tub surround.

- **RESILIENT FLOORING:** Faced with heavy competition from its ceramic, laminate, wood, and stone counterparts, resilient flooring, that is, vinyl and linoleum, has made a strong comeback with the introduction of beautiful styles and patterns.

  In addition to its good looks and durability, today's vinyl sheet flooring is surprisingly difficult to distinguish from its hard-surface lookalikes. Vinyl tile is a great option for the do-it-yourselfer and comes in a wide variety of colors and patterns. From metallics to textural crocodile patterns, you'll be amazed by the versatility of vinyl.

  Linoleum, which is comprised of linseed oil and other natural materials, is currently enjoying a resurgence of popularity. Offering a retro look, linoleum comes in vivid colors in both classic and modern styles. It's also a durable material that emits no harmful pollutants.

- **CONCRETE:** Although a driveway or retaining wall comes to mind, concrete can give a bath a very Zen-like look. This cement mixture can be infused with colors and grace walls, floors, and counters.

OPPOSITE: This sheet vinyl has a textural quality that mimics the skin of a crocodile. The result is a warm, rich, interesting floor.

BELOW: Believe it or not, these wood floors date from 1720. The Pennsylvania bath was updated, but the floors just had to be refinished.

Fabulous Fixtures

You'll find a wide array of choices in sinks, tubs, and showers. Here's a rundown of what you can expect.

- **SINKS:** For the bath, you'll find surface-mounted, under-mounted, counter-top-integrated sinks, vessels, pedestals, and consoles. Each type has advantages and disadvantages, depending on what you need and want. Surface-mounted sinks are relatively inexpensive and easy to install. Under-mounted sinks are a bit more expensive and harder to install. They fasten to the countertop on the underside, making it necessary to finish the edges of the counter opening for the sink. You'll also have to drill holes in the countertop for the faucet and spout or consider wall-mounted fittings. However, under-mounted sinks offer a more elegant look and give a smooth transition from countertop to sink. Integrated sinks, which are sold as one solid piece with the surrounding counter surface, are probably the most hygienic option. Made of solid surfacing or quartz, installation is a breeze because they are part of the counter. The only downside with integrated sinks is that you can't just replace the sink or the counter since they are a package deal. Vessel sinks, made of fireclay, stone, metal, or glass, sit on top of the counter—and really make a design statement. Pedestal and console sinks offer a more traditional look. Because consoles have a wider deck than pedestals, they are a bit more practical. If you love this look but need a place to store towels or soaps, consider a console or washstand sink that has a shelf on the bottom.

  Once you decide on your sink, you'll need to pick a faucet. You will be astounded by today's variety. The finishes range from sparkling chrome to antiqued bronze, and a few manufacturers now offer finishes that resist scratches, so your faucet will stay shiny and new. If you want a sleek

A two-story addition gave this home a spacious master bath with honed marble floors, a marble tub surround, and a bank of cabinets and drawers that provide plenty of built-in storage.

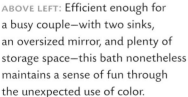

ABOVE LEFT: Efficient enough for a busy couple—with two sinks, an oversized mirror, and plenty of storage space—this bath nonetheless maintains a sense of fun through the unexpected use of color.

ABOVE RIGHT: The bathroom vanity is streamlined, yet still accommodates two people at once. Roman shades and industrial-looking light fixtures create an eclectic mix.

bath, consider a wall-mounted fixture, evoking the atmosphere of a spa. Traditionalists might stick to a classic form with old-fashioned enamel details or any of the vast array of authentic period designs now produced in quality materials.

On a practical note, when shopping for a faucet, look for quality. Solid brass is the best type of material. Other less expensive options include chrome-plated, tubular brass, and chrome plated pot metal. You will also find that there are washer and washerless faucets. Washerless faucets are preferable, because washers wear out and need replacing. Washerless faucets have the working parts in one contained cartridge which is either constructed of ceramic or plastic.

OPPOSITE: Take advantage of natural light and views by placing your bathtub in front of a low window that looks onto a private terrace or garden.

RIGHT: For this bath, the windows were intentionally placed high up, so that the room could benefit from natural light without giving up privacy. White marble and bead-board surround the tub.

• TUBS: There's something about a tub that just says luxury. And even if you take showers 90 percent of the time, it's important to include a tub in your master bathroom, because a tub will add value to your home at resale. Enameled cast-iron are the best quality tubs. However, they are extremely heavy, and you must make sure that your floor can hold one of these. For a lightweight option, consider fiberglass-reinforced acrylic. These can be molded with body-shaping forms to add comfort when you take a soak.

- **WHIRLPOOLS:** In the last few decades, whirlpools have gone from a high-end item to one that's practically standard for new houses. Keep in mind that bigger is not necessarily better. When it comes to whirlpools, the optimum soaking depth for comfort is 20 to 21 inches. If possible, try out the tub itself in the showroom. Shapes range from standard rectangles to ovals and corner units, as well as round and cloverleaf designs. Generally, tubs come with four to eight jets, the positions of which can be changed to direct the bubbling flow. Look for whirlpools with jets that are distributed throughout the tub—on both sides and at opposite ends—so that all points of your body benefit from the therapeutic effect. Also, check to make sure that all back and foot jets are recessed properly into the bath so that you can comfortably rest your body against them.

  Any whirlpool tub you purchase should carry listings for Underwriters Laboratories (UL) and the International Association of Plumbing and Mechanical Officials (IAPMO). The UL listing ensures that the electronics are fully grounded, while the IAPMO listing guarantees that the tub meets plumbing codes. For maximum safety, seek out a tub with a safety-suction system. If anything, such as jewelry or a bather's hair, gets caught in a duct, the suction system will shut off the unit immediately.

- **AIRBATHS:** Although airbaths have been around since about 1980, more and more homeowners are becoming aware of this option. These baths include tiny holes in the bottom of the tub, where puffs of air create a gentle, effervescent effect. Some manufacturers now offer a combination airbath/whirlpool tub.

An expansion allowed room for this master bath which was previously the master bedroom. The whirlpool tub was one of the homeowners' favorite additions.

A spacious shower, a dual vanity, plenty of storage, and a whirlpool bathtub with a marble surround complete this master bath. Cattails are sandwiched in the shower door glass.

- **SHOWERS:** Prefabricated units are the most affordable choice when it comes to showers. These are generally constructed of molded plastics, such as acrylic or fiberglass. With custom showers, you have a wide variety of materials from which to choose. Ceramic tile continues to be popular, however, many high-end baths now include different types of stone, from glossy marbles to textural slates. Also, concrete gives a textural quality and can be infused with color to afford a unique look. Glass block offers translucency while maintaining privacy, and glass tiles provide an updated take on a classic material.

Shower systems have become all the rage, offering multiple heads with different massaging features. These systems offer a good alternative to the whirlpool bath. With our busy lives, we want a place to relax, but we don't always have time to fill a tub. Some showers now offer steam options as well. Certainly, these features will replace the routine of your morning shower with an exhilarating experience.

- **TOILETS:** Although not the most glamorous feature in the bath, all agree with its necessity. You'll have to choose between one and two-piece units. One-piece units, also called low-profile toilets, give a sleek look and often include an elongated bowl which is easier to clean than those on two-piece units.

OPPOSITE: For the shower, the Long Island homeowner and her architect installed a handheld unit. It's not only practical, but it continues the old-fashioned scheme seen throughout the whole house.

RIGHT: The steam shower has two showerheads, and the doors and fittings are finished in nickel. Less shiny than chrome, nickel offers a refined look to the bath.

BELOW: Deep drawers in the cabinetry are a practical choice because they can accommodate a wider variety of objects. The stark white walls and cabinetry enhance the clean lines and look of this well-ordered bath.

Special Features

What will make a bath really stand out? Here's our list.

- RADIANT FLOORING: Radiant heat provides warmth underfoot. Two types of technology are available. Hydronic heating will give overall heat while electric heating offers spot warming. Talk to your builder to find out which type would be best for your project.

- TOWEL WARMERS: These racks will make your bath into a luxurious retreat. Imagine leaving your shower and enveloping yourself with a warm towel—fabulous!

- UNIQUE FEATURES: Consider unique details for your space, like hand-painted tiles. Some sinks feature hand-painted designs as well. Or on a smaller scale, purchase monogrammed towels to add a personal touch. And don't forget to carefully choose things like your soap dispenser and tissue holder.

ABOVE: Although you can't see it, this bath features radiant heating, and the homeowners of this lakeside retreat really appreciate it on cold mornings.

OPPOSITE: A large soaking tub dominates this spacious bathroom. The water for the tub streams down dramatically from the ceiling.

CHAPTER TEN

The Great Outdoors

Devising a Scheme

Looking for a change of scenery? Now's the time to get the most enjoyment from your property and engage your family in fresh-air living. The key is to expand your living areas beyond the interior rooms of your house by treating the outdoors as an extension of your home. But before you begin dreaming about relaxing in the hammock, factor the answers to these questions into your plan.

Lifestyle

- How do you use your yard now?

- How would you like to spend your time outdoors?

- Do you have large family gatherings or entertain frequently? How often? What is the size of a typical gathering?

- Do you entertain formally or informally?

A spacious balcony is set beneath a gracious archway and flanked by columns. Simple twig furnishings offer a place to sit and ponder the Wyoming landscape.

- Do you need to plan with young children or pets in mind? For example, a single-level deck might better serve a family with young children than a multilevel one.

General

- Describe your ideal outdoor space. What is the overall feeling?

- What type of outdoor activities are essential? For example, do you plan to have big barbecues? Do you want a spot to read in peace and quiet under the trees?

- What is your favorite time of day? Of the year?

Climate Considerations

- During what seasons can you use your outdoor space?

- Would the addition of an overhang extend your use of the space?

ABOVE LEFT: An outdoor "living room" features a sheltered area complete with a limestone-and-granite-faced fireplace, a table, and plenty of comfortable seating.

ABOVE RIGHT: A masonry fireplace allows homeowners and guests to stay warm even when the sun goes down. It also creates a feeling of being indoors.

OPPOSITE: Walnut travertine flooring expands the living space outdoors. A round table and chairs accommodate the family for breakfast under the open sky.

- Where will you need shade?

The View from Inside the Home

- What will the view be like from the inside looking out? (Note: Ample use of glass facing an adjoining outdoor living area such as a deck or patio visually extends your indoor living area.)

- What will be the focal point to pull you out into the landscape? A gazebo or a fireplace?

Once you've answered these questions, you can determine what type of space will be right for you. For example, if you love to entertain outdoors, you'll need a large enough area to accommodate your guests, plus seating areas, and cooking gear. If you spend your time reading a book in the shade, perhaps a covered porch would work well for your needs.

ABOVE: A cozy terrace includes a walled-in private retreat with a spa. An abundance of greenery softens the look of the concrete wall.

LEFT: What makes this setting spectacular? Certainly the canyon views, but also the vanishing-edge pool and the native stone that surrounds the pool and adorns an adjoining patio.

OPPOSITE: The balcony wraps around the corner of the house, offering a spectacular panoramic view of the Colorado mountaintops. Copper-clad windows will weather gracefully with age.

Options in Decks

Outdoor decks have become an important element to many homes. While their appeal is widespread, so is the selection of decking materials. In the last few years alone, options have expanded to include a host of high-tech materials and exotic woods from around the world. As a result, selecting the material that's right for you is often a daunting task. Below, we take you through the pros and cons of different materials.

- **WOOD MATERIALS:** Most would agree that wood offers the most visually appealing surface of any deck material. Its characteristic beauty is a natural bond to our outdoor environment. Yet, all this beauty comes with a price. Depending on the climate and type of wood, most wood decks must be power-washed, stained, and resealed every one to three years.

  Softwoods like pine and Douglas fir are the least expensive material among the most readily available. However, they have a shorter lifespan than other products. Changes in temperature and moisture can cause the wood to crack, split, and warp, or splinter unless regularly maintained. Quality cedar and redwood are less likely to splinter and are naturally resistant to moisture and decay, but they are still subject to denting and marring.

ABOVE LEFT: Durable and beautiful, the rich qualities of western red cedar make a great impression.

ABOVE RIGHT: This decking is made from cedar that is less likely to splinter than materials like pine and Douglas fir and is naturally resistant to moisture and decay.

Premium hardwoods, such as Ipe (also called ironwood) can easily last a lifetime. Extreme density and tight graining make it harder than softwoods, stronger than plastic decking, and very low maintenance. Sealers aren't necessary except to maintain the original color. Initial costs of premium hardwoods are comparable to quality cedar, redwood, and composite material, however, the labor costs to build your deck can be higher since the wood is harder to work with.

- **MAN-MADE MATERIALS:** Though they lack the true character of wood, today's man-made products have made decks nearly maintenance-free. What are the negatives? Lighter-colored decks may cause glare and treated lumber joists and beams sometimes make a deck feel as though it bounces a bit. Your options in man-made materials consist of composites, a recycled material made of wood fibers and plastic; plastics, usually comprised of recycled milk jugs; and aluminum.

RIGHT: Made from 100 percent recycled materials of wood fibers and recycled polyethylene, this composite surface is virtually waterproof and never needs treating or sealing.

BELOW: The vinyl deck is made from PVC vinyl, a material that withstands harsh weather, so it's great for places that have extreme climates.

Composite decking installs and weathers like wood although it lacks its strength. These decks are dimensionally consistent, slip-resistant and durable; plus they won't splinter, rot, warp, dent, or crack. Most products will eventually weather to a shade of gray, though some companies now offer a new line of wood-look hues protected by UV stabilizers to keep colors from fading.

Plastics hold their color for many years, and they don't require sanding, sealing, or staining. Prices vary, though they're often slightly higher than redwood, cedar, and most composites. PVC vinyl is a rigid plastic that holds up to harsh weather conditions without peeling, blistering, rotting or splintering. The non-slip surface is said to remain cool even during the hottest days of summer. Color choices are minimal (usually white, gray, or beige) and so is maintenance—just hose down to clean.

If you're looking for a product that will really last for many years, consider aluminum. This material usually comes with a lifetime warranty. However, it's often costly and can be difficult to cut.

Composite decking cuts, drills, and fastens like wood, but the product contains no knots and never rots, splinters, or splits.

For a more natural, rustic look in the yard, try irregular-shaped pieces of granite. This meandering walkway complements the natural landscape.

Perfect Patios

Depending on the design of your home, you may choose to extend your living areas outdoors by including a patio. Patios can be made of brick, gravel, concrete, or stone pavers, and you can get a variety of looks with each. A tumbled stone patio, for example, will give a European flavor to your backyard, while concrete pavers in a diamond pattern with alternating colors appeal to the modern aesthetic. When selecting a material for your patio, the key is a patio that blends with the architecture of the house. Another major consideration is the climate where you live. Concrete will withstand the freeze-thaw cycle well, and for that reason it's a good underlayer for such natural stones as bluestone or granite laid with mortar joints. Natural stone can also be laid on

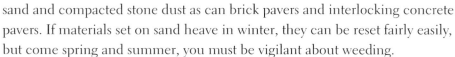

sand and compacted stone dust as can brick pavers and interlocking concrete pavers. If materials set on sand heave in winter, they can be reset fairly easily, but come spring and summer, you must be vigilant about weeding.

You will also need to decide on the shape of the patio. Will it have a curved edge or do you prefer a more rigid geometry? You may want a low wall surrounding the patio where family and friends can sit and enjoy views of your garden. How will the adjacent area to the patio be landscaped? Incorporating potted plants is a great way to have instant foliage around your patio. Placed along the edges, the plants can soften the look of, say, a concrete patio.

Finally, think about what's overhead. A roof not only provides shelter, it adds structure and style to the setting. Roofs can vary from pergolas and gazebos to a canvas umbrella.

OPPOSITE, FAR LEFT: If you want a subtle look for your patio with a hint of color, consider bluestone. Here in Rhode Island, the architect employed the material amidst boulders and plantings.

OPPOSITE, TOP: In Silver Spring, Maryland, the flagstone used in this patio and hillside entrance bestows a country atmosphere in this bustling suburb of Washington, D.C.

OPPOSITE, CENTER: Accessorize your patio with decorative planters. Planters come in a variety of sizes and colors, and are an easy way to add attractive details to a yard.

OPPOSITE, BOTTOM: Made of concrete, these diamond-shaped black-and-white veined pavers are hand-packed into molds to create a unique look.

RIGHT: Although it looks like stone, this is actually stamped concrete. With such a precise imitation, the concrete tiles might fool even your savviest guest.

THE GREAT OUTDOORS

On the Porch

Porches evoke a sense of easy living. You simply can't be stressed out when you're sitting on a swing or reading a book in a rocking chair on your covered porch. A porch also offers a place to get outdoors when the weather is not cooperating, and screened porches are especially versatile. Just like a deck or patio, the architecture of your house will dictate the type of porch you should create. Talk to your builder about the orientation of the porch. If he or she is from the area where you live, he should understand the exigencies of your climate. If you live in Arizona for instance, you don't want a south-facing porch, as it will get too much sun. Once the porch is on your floor plan, you'll need to think about materials. Most porches are constructed of wood, but you may select man-made products or wood for the millwork. Man-made detailing is usually less expensive than wood and is resistant to rot and decay.

OPPOSITE: An arbor above the poolside patio provides more than shade—it also serves as a visual connection between the outdoor spaces and the house.

BELOW: There's nothing like sitting on a rocking chair on the front porch to remind us of days gone by—and it's only a matter of time before Mom comes out with the homemade apple pie.

The soaring screened porch, an
addition to the early eighteenth-
century home, provides a wonderful
gathering place for the homeowners
and their guests.

Outdoor Kitchens

Once you've created your outdoor space, think about dining al fresco. With the many innovative products on the market, your outdoor prep area can be sophisticated enough to let you create elegant gourmet feasts—as well as those tried-and-true grilled dinners.

When planning an outdoor kitchen, consider available area and good placement. The size of the kitchen will be determined by how much you want to include and how elaborate it will be, anywhere from a 5 x 5-foot corner to a 20 x 20-foot culinary center. For convenience, position it just beyond the indoor kitchen or family room. Provide a natural transition from the indoors to the outdoors with a large sliding door or multiple French doors. Take note: Make sure your location can support the weight of the appliances you plan to include. Choose weatherproof materials for cabinetry, counters, sink, and exposed fixtures. Slate, teak, stainless steel, and stone are clearly good options.

If you decide a small built-in grill and storage cabinet will suffice, you may be able to install them yourself. However, if you're going all out, seek the advice of a qualified professional, such as a certified kitchen designer and rely on licensed contractors for installation of electrical and gas connections. For safety, insist on ground fault interrupters (GFIs) for all electrical runs.

Regarding appliances, almost everything that you can have inside you can now have outside. So where to begin? Purchase the best grill that you can afford. This will serve as the centerpiece for your outdoor kitchen. You'll find both freestanding and built-in models in gas, charcoal, and electric (for flame-restricted areas). Some grills will even offer the flexibility of switching from gas to charcoal.

Features for grills include side burners, griddles, woks, and motorized rotisseries. Moveable grilling grids that can be adjusted to different heights are a convenient option. And if you love a true smoky flavor, select a grill with a built-in wood-chip tray. Grills range from a few hundred dollars for a basic portable unit to several thousand dollars and up for a top-of-the-line, built-in model. Price will depend on the size of the grilling surface and number of BTUs (if gas) of the unit.

Once you've selected your grill, consider a refrigerator for your outdoor space. These are usually small, under-the-counter models, and for safety and maintenance reasons, are made of stainless steel with a water-resistant thermostat, sealed electrical contacts, and insulated electrical terminals. Models

range from $300 to $500 and up. Manufacturers now offer other products specifically designed for the outdoors, such as dishwashers, wine coolers, beer dispensers, ice makers, warming drawers, and trash compactors.

Keep in mind, whatever elements you choose, you're sure to have plenty of great dining experiences. Just be sure to check the weather channel before you plan your party.

A metal table and chairs give homeowners the durability they need as well as a stylish look. Brightly colored teacups add a hint of color as does the potted plant.

Fully Furnished

Bring the indoors out with comfortable furniture that's as appealing to sit on as it is to look at. A cushioned sofa or chair upholstered in weather-resistant fabric should stand up to the outdoor elements. For the framework, choose sensible materials, such as weather-resistant wicker or metal that won't rust.

If you have a covered porch or patio, consider a daybed or futon to provide a spot for a midday nap. Plenty of weather-resistant throw pillows will also add comfort. And be sure to include accessories, such as a rubberized rug or painted floorcloth. Decorate your outdoor room with a unique assortment of items made from stone, ceramic, iron, or terra-cotta. Include colorful hanging baskets and a variety of potted plants set at different heights. You'll soon discover an environment that beckons you to come out, and ultimately, just may become your favorite place to be.

OPPOSITE: Family and guests can choose from several sitting areas on the porch. Set atop plank flooring, which resists fading and requires no maintenance, the cushioned sofas and chairs feature a cheerful striped fabric.

ABOVE: Adirondack-style chairs in bright colors are lined up on the porch. For this lakeside property they provide plenty of seating and a touch of whimsy at the same time.

CHAPTER ELEVEN

Plans

Reading Architectural Drawings

When designing your home, you'll be faced with a number of architectural drawings. They may be in blueprint form or on vellum, a translucent piece of paper. To some people, reading these drawings is simple, while many others feel overwhelmed when their builder first shows his or her plans. To start, here are the different types of drawings you may see.

- **FLOOR PLAN:** This is a flat look at your home. You're looking at your home from above. All the plumbing fixtures and appliances will generally be drawn in, so you can see their placement in the scheme. floor plans are drawn to scale. Generally, the scale is listed at the bottom of the drawing. For example, a plan may be drawn at ¼-inch scale. What this means is that each ¼-inch on the plan is 1 foot in reality. A 4-foot wall, for instance, will be 1 inch long on the drawing.

Recessed into the footprint of the house instead of tacked onto the side of it, the porch is a graceful and integral aspect of the home's design.

Strong materials, such as stainless steel, stone, glass, and wood, lend interest and grace to oversized spaces and soaring ceilings.

- **ELEVATION:** These drawings are generally used to show details. They are a vertical rendition of a structure. You might see elevations in order for your architect or builder to show you what the exterior of your house will look like. You will be able to see things like brickwork, windowsills, shutters, and door styles in exterior elevations. For interior elevations, you can see things like the placement of kitchen and bathroom cabinets, laundry areas, fireplaces, bookcases, and other built-ins. Little extras, such as a mantelpiece and wainscoting, plus molding sections, provide details that give your home a custom look.

- **SECTIONAL:** Sectionals are similar to elevations, however, these drawings are done as if you cut through the house and are looking at a portion of the house at a given point. With a sectional you will see a cut line, and you may even see where the 2 x 4 is placed within a wall. Although this is still a two-dimensional drawing, you can tell how spaces are layered. For example, you'll see that an island is set in front of a sink area, even though its proximity won't be apparent. Thus, you will be able to see how the various parts of the house fit together.

This old-fashioned screened porch has heavy, glass-paneled doors surrounded by teak that fold out like an accordion. When the weather warms up, the doors are folded into two hidden closets, one of which is seen here to the left of the screen. When it cools down, the doors pull out on a track for instant glass walls. The space is heated by cast-iron radiators during the winter.

- AXONOMETRIC: This type of drawing allows homeowners to really get a bird's eye view of a space. Axonometrics are generally quite impressive. They look like a drawing of a model. However, truth be told, they are very easily done. Axons, as they are often called, are created by placing the floor plan on a 45-degree angle and drawing upward. If you're working with an architect, he or she may create this drawing for you, but most blueprints that are bought as a package do not include this type of drawing.

PLANS

LEFT: The guest room's cathedral ceiling was added to this home during a renovation, creating a light and airy ambiance to the room.

ABOVE: This dining room table is actually an extension of a second, small kitchen island to the right. Cabinets form the base of the island at one end of the dining table. The chairs deliberately don't match.

LEFT: If you enjoy entertaining, be sure to consider a well-designed bar with ample storage space for stemware, wine, beer, and other bar supplies. This expansive bar features a built-in wine rack, under-counter refrigerator, icemaker, and sink.

BELOW: In warm weather regions, consider features that allow indoor and outdoor spaces to merge. Here, sliding glass doors hide in a wall pocket. When open, they increase the space available for entertaining.

- **PERSPECTIVE:** Aptly named, these drawings give perspective to the room to help homeowners to get a sense of the space. Perspectives can be simple black-and-white line drawings, or they can be artfully rendered to offer a crystal clear look at an area.

Now that you know the different types of drawings, here are some basic forms that will be included in a floor plan.

- **DOORS:** You can identify these by looking for a D-shaped form. The flat part of the form is the actual opening, while the curved area defines the door swing, so you can tell if the door swings outward or into the room. Front doors generally measure about 3 feet wide, while interior doors are about 2 to 2½ feet wide. Double doors will look like the letter B, showing two door swings. Pocket doors are a bit harder to detect, but these will be shown with multiple straight lines with one line fitting into two lines, which signifies the door receding into the wall.

- **WALLS:** Generally, these are denoted with a solid black line.

- **ROOFLINES:** In some plans, a dotted line is used to show the roof. This will also let you know how the ceiling is shaped. For example, some master bedrooms include a tray ceiling. This will be drawn with four dotted lines extending from the corners of a square or rectangle (also dotted lines).

In a nod to Thomas Jefferson, an idol of the homeowner, the sweeping staircase was modeled after the one at Monticello, making the entrance hall one of the grandest areas in the home.

- **WINDOWS:** Look for spots where the solid lines are broken with a thin rectangle, composed of three horizontal lines. The three lines denote the window panes. You should also be able to tell how many windows are next to one another on a given wall. A bay window will extend beyond the exterior wall; picture windows will not show any markings and will include unbroken lines, showing the length of the glazing.

- **STAIRS:** Multiple lines will depict the steps. Often, you'll see an arrow or the words "up" or "down." This will let you know whether the steps lead to an upper or lower level. Landings should be drawn in. Just keep in mind that these drawings represent a flattened version of the actual stair viewed from above.

- **CLOSETS:** Often marked "CL," squares or rectangles will depict a closet. A plan will also tell you what kind of closet you have: The abbreviation, WIC, stands for walk-in closet and LIN for a linen closet. Utility closets may be marked as well. Doors also will be clearly drawn: those that swing into the room, bifolds, or doors on a track.

- **FIREPLACES:** These usually look like rectangles with a bite in them. In some cases, the letters FP are marked on the floor plan.

PLANS

OPPOSITE: For the electrical plan of this great room, the architect had to consider all the appliances, the various pendant lights, as well as power for the ceiling fan.

RIGHT: In a house built by a sea captain more than 200 years ago, a new pass-through contains a rack on which to hang glasses, a nod to the careful space planning onboard boats. The pass-through connects the kitchen to the living room, increasing the sense of space.

- **POSTS AND COLUMNS:** These are shown with a square, rectangle, or circle, depending on the shape of your post.

- **SINKS:** Basically, this should look like the sink you'll be getting. If you have a double sink slated for the kitchen, you should see a drawing that includes two basins. You may also see the difference between a sink set in a vanity versus a pedestal sink.

- **SHOWERS:** Generally, these are shown with a box with an X through it.

- **TUBS AND TOILETS:** These should be fairly obvious when you see them in the bathroom.

- **ISLANDS AND PENINSULAS:** Denoted with a thinner line than those used for the walls, you'll be able to tell where these units are located within the kitchen.

- **DISHWASHERS:** These will be drawn to scale and denoted with a dotted line if a countertop covers them. Sometimes marked "DW."

When designing a living room it's important to create conversation areas. Here, two wing chairs cozy up to a sofa. Each has its own side table to place a glass of water or cup of tea.

- **REFRIGERATORS:** Generally, a square or rectangular shape is drawn. Sometimes the door will be depicted with an extra line. In some cases, this is marked with an X.

- **COOKTOPS:** The number of burners is made evident by circles drawn within a rectangular shape.

- **WASHERS AND DRYERS:** Often marked "W" and "D," these are drawn to scale. If they are beneath a counter, they will be depicted with a dotted line instead of a solid one.

This home's simple shed-roof design directs views toward Sun Valley, Idaho vistas; the terrace extends from the main living area. The siding is mahogany-stained Douglas fir.

Purchasing House Plans

There are a number of companies that offer architectural plans for your dream home. Generally, sets include a sketch of the exterior of the home to give you a sense of what it will look like; foundation plans, including support walls, excavated and unexcavated areas, if any; and foundation notes, detailed floor plans of each level, house cross-sections, and interior and exterior elevations.

For an additional fee you can also get the following documents to complement your blueprints:

- PLUMBING: Most blueprint packages include locations for all the plumbing fixtures, including sinks, lavatories, tubs, showers, toilets, laundry tubs, and water heaters, but if you want to know more about the complete plumbing system, consider purchasing the extra documents. Look for plans that have been prepared to meet the requirements of the National Plumbing Code. They should show you such useful information as pipe schedules, fittings, sump-pump details, water-softener hookups, and septic system details.

LEFT: Dubbed the Temple Bar because of its classical columns, the outdoor bar includes refrigerators, a sink, and a television. The plumbing plan was carefully thought out when the architect designed this bar.

BELOW: Carriage lanterns line the exterior of the house. Archways, a brick path, and a picket fence lend plenty of charm to this New Jersey home.

- **ELECTRICAL:** These should include wire sizing, switch installation schematics, cable-routing details, appliance wattage, doorbell hookups, as well as typical service panel circuitry. You'll want to get a package that meets the requirements of the National Electrical Code.

- **CONSTRUCTION:** This depicts the materials and methods to build foundations, fireplaces, walls, floors, and roofs. Where appropriate, some kits will offer alternative construction methods.

- **MECHANICAL:** For fundamental principles and useful data that will help you make informed decisions and communicate with subcontractors about heating and cooling systems, you might consider purchasing a mechanical detail set.

- **SPECIFICATION OUTLINE:** This document should list critical stages and crucial items for the building process. It is a document that can be filled out by you or your builder to make sure you get every detail right. When combined with blueprints, a signed contract, and a schedule, the specification outline becomes a legal document and record for the building of your home.

- **FURNITURE PLANNER:** Often these packages include either peel-and-stick renditions of furnishings or templates to allow you to draw in furnishings where you want them. This allows you to try different layouts for each room, without moving heavy furniture.

COPYRIGHT DOS AND DON'TS

Blueprints for residential construction (or working drawings, as they are often called in the industry) are copyrighted intellectual property, protected under the terms of the United States Copyright Law, and therefore, cannot be copied legally for use in building. However, here is a list of guidelines to help you obtain the right number of copies of a chosen blueprint design.

Copyright Dos

- **Do** purchase enough copies of the blueprints to satisfy building requirements. As a rule for a home or project plan you will need a set for yourself, two or three for your builder and subcontractors, two for the local building department, and one to three for your mortgage

When planning your ideal house, make sure you go through all the proper channels. If you take all the right steps, you're certain to turn dreams into realities as the owners of this Colonial Revival house did.

lender. You may want to check with your local building department or your builder to see how many they need before your purchase. You may need to buy eight to ten sets; note that some areas of the country require purchase of vellums (also called repro-ducibles) instead of blueprints. Vellums can be written on and changed more easily than blue-prints. Also, keep in mind that plans are only good for one-time construction.

- **Do** consider reverse blueprints if you want to flop the floor plan. Lettering and numbering will appear backward, but the reversed sets will help you and your builder better visualize the design.

- **Do** take advantage of multiple set discounts at the time you place your order. Usually, purchasing additional sets after you receive your initial order is not cost-effective.

- **Do** take advantage of vellums. Though they are a little more expen-sive, they can be changed, copied, and used for one-time construction of a home. You will receive a copyright release letter with your vellums that will allow you to have them copied.

- **Do** talk with a professional service representative before placing your order. They can give you great advice about what packages are avail-able for your chosen design and what will work best for your particu-lar situation.

For their second-floor master bedroom, white surfaces from top to bottom magnify light, creating a bright and airy look the owners were seeking. Windows opposite the bed have ocean views.

TOP LEFT: What could be better than having a sauna in your home? Lined in western red cedar and heated by rocks, this sauna provides a host of therapeutic benefits.

TOP RIGHT: Designed to resemble a traditional sleeping porch, the sunroom, which does double duty as an office, is clad in fir paneling.

BOTTOM LEFT: Even your laundry room can be special. Here, an ironing cabinet allows the board to be neatly stowed away, and handy drawers under the washer and dryer give extra storage and raise up units for easy access.

BOTTOM RIGHT: For a mud room the architect custom-made a closet system for storing hats, scarves, and even shoes; plus he included a bench for gearing up for the outdoors.

PLANS

Copyright Don'ts

- **DON'T** think you should purchase only one set of blueprints for a building project. One is fine if you want to study the plan closely, but will not be enough for actual building.

- **DON'T** expect your builder or a copy center to make copies of standard blueprints. They cannot do so legally and most copy centers are aware of this.

- **DON'T** purchase standard blueprints if you know you'll want to make changes to the plans; vellums are a better value.

- **DON'T** use blueprints or vellums more than one time. Additional fees apply if you want to build more than one time from a set of drawings.

TOP LEFT: Designed as the hearth of the house, the kitchen includes a six-sided maple island that has a granite top and space for plenty of family and friends to congregate.

TOP RIGHT: Only the best appliances were chosen for this New Jersey kitchen. The top-of-the-line wine cooler fits neatly in the island.

ABOVE: Enveloped in walnut cabinetry, the six-burner cooktop serves a big family well. Corbels and rope molding are just a few of the intricate details used in the space.

ABOVE: Hardy perennials, which provide cover and food for birds, are artfully arranged to soften the edges of the slate walkway.

RIGHT: With a Mediterranean aura, the private third-floor balcony provides the best views in this house on the New Jersey shore.

Photography Credits

Page 114: Sam Gray

Page 115: Tony Giammarino

Page 116 (top left): Lydia Gould Bessler

Page 116 (top right): Tony Giammarino

Page 116 (bottom): Sam Gray

Page 117: Sam Gray

Page 118: Sam Gray

Page 119: James Yochum

Page 120: Sam Gray

Page 121 (top): Mark Samu

Page 121 (bottom): Tony Giammarino

Page 122: Lydia Gould Bessler

Page 124 (top): Sam Gray

Page 124 (bottom): Sam Gray

Page 125: Sam Gray

Page 127: John Bessler

Page 128 (top): Jason McConathy

Page 128 (bottom): Jason McConathy

Page 129: Jason McConathy

Page 130: Jason McConathy

Page 131 (left): Jason McConathy

Page 131 (right): Mark Samu

Page 132 (left): John Bessler

Page 132 (right): Mark Samu

Page 133 (top): Mark Samu

Page 133 (bottom): Sam Gray

Page 134 (left): Tony Giammarino

Page 134 (right): Tony Giammarino

Page 135: Jason McConathy

Page 136 (left): Courtesy of Hunter Douglas

Page 136 (right): Courtesy of Smith + Noble

Page 137: Mark Samu

Page 138 (left): Courtesy of Grammercy

Page 138 (right): Courtesy of Grammercy

Page 139: Sam Gray

Page 141: Mark Samu

Page 142: Sam Gray

Page 144 (left): Sam Gray

Page 144 (right): Sam Gray

Page 145: Tony Giammarino

Page 146 (left): Jason McConathy

Page 146 (right): Jason McConathy

Page 147: Jason McConathy

Page 148: Sam Gray

Page 149: Sam Gray

Page 150: Sam Gray

Page 151: Courtesy of Bassett Furniture

Page 152: Courtesy of Garnet Hill

Page 153: Sam Gray

Page 154 (top): Jason McConathy

Page 154 (bottom): Grey Crawford

Page 155: Grey Crawford

Page 156: Courtesy of Ladd Furniture

Page 157 (top left): Courtesy of The Land of Nod

Page 157 (bottom left): Courtesy of Congoleum

Page 157 (right): Courtesy of Waverly

Page 158: Sam Gray

Page 159: Sam Gray

Page 160: Jason McConathy

Page 162: Bill Holt

Page 163: Bill Geddes

Page 164: Doug Walker

Page 165 (left): Mark Samu

Page 165 (right): Sam Gray

Page 166: Courtesy of Armstrong

Page 167: Julie Semel

Page 168: Peter Loppacher

Page 169 (left): Mark Lohman

Page 169 (right): Mark Samu

Page 170: Peter Loppacher

Page 171: James Yochum

Page 172: Mark Samu

Page 173: Mark Samu

Page 174: Mark Samu

Page 174 (left): Sam Gray

Page 175 (right): Sam Gray

Page 176: Sam Gray

Page 177: Peter Loppacher

Page 178: Jason McConathy

Page 180 (left): Lydia Gould Bessler

Page 180 (right): Lydia Gould Bessler

Page 181: Lydia Gould Bessler

Page 182 (top): Lydia Gould Bessler

Page 182 (bottom): Courtesy of National Spa & Pool Institute

Page 183: Jason McConathy

Page 184 (left): Courtesy of Weyerhaeuser

Page 184 (right): Courtesy of Weyerhaeuser

Page 185 (left): Courtesy of Dream Deck Vinyl Deck

Page 185 (right): Courtesy of ChoiceDek

Page 186: Courtesy of Weatherbest

Page 187: Philip Jensen-Carter; Courtesy of Jane Didona

Page 188 (left): Courtesy of © Katherine Field and Associates

Page 188 (top right): Courtesy of Jeff Goldman and Associates

Page 188 (middle right): Courtesy of Pavestone

Page 188 (bottom right): Courtesy of Buddy Rhodes

Page 189: Courtesy of Increte Systems

Page 190: Mark Samu

Page 191: Peter Loppacher

Page 192: Julie Semel

Page 194: Courtesy of KitchenAid

Page 195: Ken Gutmaker

Page 196: Sam Gray

Page 197: Mark Samu

Page 198: Sam Gray

Page 200: Fred Housel

Page 201: Peter Loppacher

Page 202: Julie Semel

Page 203: Mark Samu

Page 204 (left): Langdon Clay

Page 204 (right): Sam Gray

Page 205: Peter Loppacher

Page 206: Mark Samu

Page 207: Sam Gray

Page 208: © Robert Milliman

Page 209: Mark Samu

Page 210: Sam Gray

Page 211: Roger Wade

Page 212 (left): Peter Loppacher

Page 212 (right): Peter Loppacher

Page 213: Sam Gray

Page 214: Sam Gray

Page 215 (top left): Sam Gray

Page 215 (bottom left): Sam Gray

Page 215 (top right): Sam Gray

Page 215 (bottom left): Sam Gray

Page 216 (left): Lydia Gould Bessler

Page 216 (top right): Lydia Gould Bessler

Page 216 (bottom right): Lydia Gould Bessler

Pagd 217 (left): John Bessler

Page 217 (right): John Bessler

Index